CLAYS OF BUNGAY

CLAYS OF BUNGAY

by

JAMES MORAN

Charles John Clay

Published by
RICHARD CLAY & CO. LTD.
Bungay, Suffolk

ISBN 0 9506104 0 2 (HARDBACK)
ISBN 0 9506104 1 0 (PAPERBACK)

Set in Monotype Bembo at Bungay
and printed by litho at
Fletcher & Son Ltd Norwich,
Bound at Bungay

Contents

List of Illustrations

Acknowledgements

IN ANY HISTORICAL or biographical review it is necessary to call upon the knowledge and expertise of many individuals. Our thanks must therefore go to the late James Moran, who, with the help of the St Bride's Printing Library, carried out all the main research work and gave continual help during the final preparation of the book. We would also like to express our thanks to another author and journalist, Eric Fowler, who carried out a great deal of local background work and research, which helped enormously. To Harold Murby, who undertook the main job of editor and book planner, and to Richard Clay IV, who undertook the writing of two of the final chapters grateful thanks. Finally, we are indebted to Brooke Crutchley (lately printer to the Cambridge University Press) who so kindly agreed to write the Foreword.

JOHN M. CLAY

Foreword

I HAVE THREE powerful reasons for welcoming the opportunity to contribute a foreword to this book. When I joined the Cambridge University Press in 1930 there were many men there who had known John Clay as University Printer and not a few who had served under his father, Charles John. Secondly, throughout my own term as Printer there was close contact between the University Press and Clays of Bungay, and the most friendly of personal relations. And thirdly, the history of the printing trade in this country, with its varied fortunes, its heroes and its traditions, has fascinated me ever since I was caught up in it myself. Clays are part of that history.

Every industry worth its salt is convinced of its importance to society, and book printers pride themselves on the role they play in the cultural life of the country. Since the publishing trade assumed a separate existence, inserting itself between author and printer and between printer and reading public, the identity of printing firms has been generally obscured. But can there be anyone who reads books who has failed to notice how often the name of Clay figures in the imprint; or who has not heard of the kernless '*f*' which helped to unmask the villainies of Thomas J. Wise? Within the narrower world of book printers and publishers the firm of Clays knows the highest respect, and despite its years (now a hundred at Bungay and another fifty before that at various addresses in London), it seems to enjoy perpetual youth – vigorous, enterprising and always maintaining the highest standards of quality and service.

Personal biographies constitute one of the oldest of literary forms. Company biographies are comparatively new and have their own special interest. James Moran's account of the house of Clay seems to me a worthy example of the *genre*, and I know that it will be widely read.

BROOKE CRUTCHLEY

CHAPTER ONE

Prelude

FEW, IF ANY, human institutions spring into being without some definable origins and this is particularly true of the printing house of Clay. Its roots go deep into the history of printing technique and its own history is worthy of record because it has maintained for more than 150 years of existence the same attachment to progress with which it began. It consequently provides an intimate picture of the effects of that technical progress on a particular firm, which is sometimes more revealing than a general survey of the industry as a whole.

Clays of Bungay (the Chaucer Press) is a printing firm widely respected in the world of books, yet it did not begin its life in Bungay, the small Suffolk town with which it is now associated, but in the heart of the City of London. Moreover, members of the Clay family of printers have in the past been associated with the University Press at Cambridge where, in fact, the founder of the line began as an apprentice in 1803.

Complementary to the record of technical development is that of the firm's urge towards specialisation. Because of the many-sided nature of printing, a growing business has often found it difficult to decide in which field to concentrate – books, newspapers, periodicals, 'jobbing', posters or packaging and the various associated processes. This is an understandable dilemma – firms with modest beginnings as they expand do not like to jettison the smaller orders from old and faithful customers, but what was once a valuable order can become an embarrassment and a source of loss. The Clay firm was not immune from this problem, but all the time there is noticeable a definite tendency towards the ultimate decision – to become the large-scale book manufacturer it is today, eschewing periodical production and general jobbing work. How this came about provides additionally a case-study of the economic change in the structure of the printing industry.

While Clays were in the mainstream of technical and economic development they were also concerned with the nature of the finished product and they were consequently very much bound up with trends and fashions in the design and production of books. Moreover, since it is often difficult to separate the history of printing from that of publishing it will be found that Clays were and are an integral part of the development of British publishing.

Clays have other claims on the attention of the historian. They have been at the centre of intriguing *causes célèbre*, not the least of which was the printing of *Alice in Wonderland*, and what seems to be the serial story of that fabricator of first editions – Thomas J. Wise. These involvements were not purely fortuitous but arose from the technical ability of the firm and, in the case of Wise, from its earlier history.

Before Richard Clay, the first printer of that name, there were others, both his own forebears in the genetical sense and his predecessors as craftsmen and inventors. Just as the genes of his parents and his childhood environment helped to shape his future so did the activities of early technical pioneers, including an unlikely figure – the third Earl Stanhope. It was an indirect consequence of Stanhope's investigations into stereotyping that Clays, by a chain of circumstances, eventually settled in Bungay.

Despite enquiries carried out by members of the family in the nineteenth century the origin of the Clays, with whom this book is concerned, cannot be traced back with certainty beyond Thomas Clay (born 1726–7), who settled in Cambridge as a young man. Family tradition states that he came from Lincolnshire, the son of a farmer, that his Quaker mother died young, and that on his father marrying again Thomas, who did not get on with his stepmother, left home for Cambridge. In 1865 Betsy Coe, housekeeper of Thomas's son, John, was questioned by C. J. Clay, and she not only adhered to this story but added that Thomas Clay had worked in a grocer's shop. He lived, she said, in 'Lutt's house on the Parade next to Mr Bishop's old place, the other corner of St Edward's Passage'. The parish register for St Edward's was examined at the same time and it showed that Thomas Clay married Ann Barker of Bene't Street on April 3rd 1753. He died on March 6th 1783 and his wife on November 29th 1786, and both were buried in St Edward's churchyard. Of nine children only two grew to adulthood, of whom one, John, concerns this history. He was born in 1758 and was the father of Richard, the first printer.

John Clay married Mary Hodges of Dover on January 3rd 1784 at St Edward's Church. He kept a school for boys (known as Clay's School) in a small house on Peas Hill at the extreme end of a passage about four houses from St Edward's Passage.

John and Mary Clay had a large family (at least ten children) of whom only two, Richard (born 1789) and Percival (born 1800) lived to a ripe age. Percival went to London and became a merchant. He frequently went on voyages to Spain and Portugal, but kept in touch with his brother Richard and had some financial dealings with him. A bachelor, he died in October 1876. The tiny house in Peas Hill was very crowded with the Clay children and the pupils. Richard Clay told his grand-daughter, Mary Aimée, that his own room was so small that he was obliged to dress on his bed. A pupil of Clay's school, Thomas Case, wrote to C. J. Clay in 1899 giving some recollections of his old master. He said: 'I remember my old Master Clay as a kindly elderly man, and one can see him with his white head and spectacles as he was almost invariably occupied (during writing time) in responding to the various complaints of the boys as to "Please sir, my pen splutters . . ." ' John Clay acted as vestry clerk at the Church for more than fifty years, and in 1833 the parishioners presented him with a silver vase.

John Clay was a book-lover and a member of the Cambridge Book Club, otherwise known as the 'Bull Book Club', which had been established in 1784. It met weekly at the Bull Inn and possessed a library of more than two thousand volumes. He was also a public-spirited man and when the government of the town was re-organised in 1835 under the Municipal Corporation Act he was elected one of the six councillors for Market Ward. In the end, however, he was the victim of reform. Late in life he found that attendance in the school had fallen, and so he supplemented his income with an office in connection with the Poor Laws. In 1836 the fourteen parishes of the borough were united to form a union for the administration of the laws, which meant a loss of office for John Clay. Writing in March 1836 to his son Percival, he says: 'The operation of the Poor Law Bill will materially affect me. The Commissioners are expected to form a Union here at Lady Day; my school producing but little, and the loss of my office will reduce my income below the means of keeping house.' The letter reached his other son, Richard, who was by then established in London, and the old man was invited to live with him. He left Cambridge in the course of 1836, taking with him his housekeeper, Betsy Coe, and spent the remainder of his life under Richard's roof, where he made himself useful by teaching arithmetic to his grandchildren. He died on February 17th 1841, aged 83, and was buried in St Nicolas Cole Abbey in the City.

Richard was the third child of John and Mary Clay and was born on July 18th 1789, being educated at Dr Perse's School, in Free School Lane. In 1803 an important decision was made for the boy. He was apprenticed to Richard Watts, who was the University Printer at the time. Since the Clay house in Peas Hill, the Printer's house on the corner of Queens' Lane and Silver Street (where the Printing house itself stood), Dr Perse's School and the Bull Inn[1] were all within a few minutes walk of each other, the paths of the vestry clerk and the Printer must have often crossed.[2] The apprenticeship could have been the outcome of a discussion between Clay and Watts about the boy's future. Little could any of them have realised that Richard Clay's own son and grandsons would occupy the position of University Printers, indeed being the last to be 'admitted into partnership' with the University; on the death of one of the grandsons, John, in 1916 the idea of a partnership with an outside printer was dropped in favour of a staff appointment. Nor could any of the participants in the apprenticeship agreement have visualised the eventual outcome. There could have been few outlets for a boy of Richard's position at that time in the small world

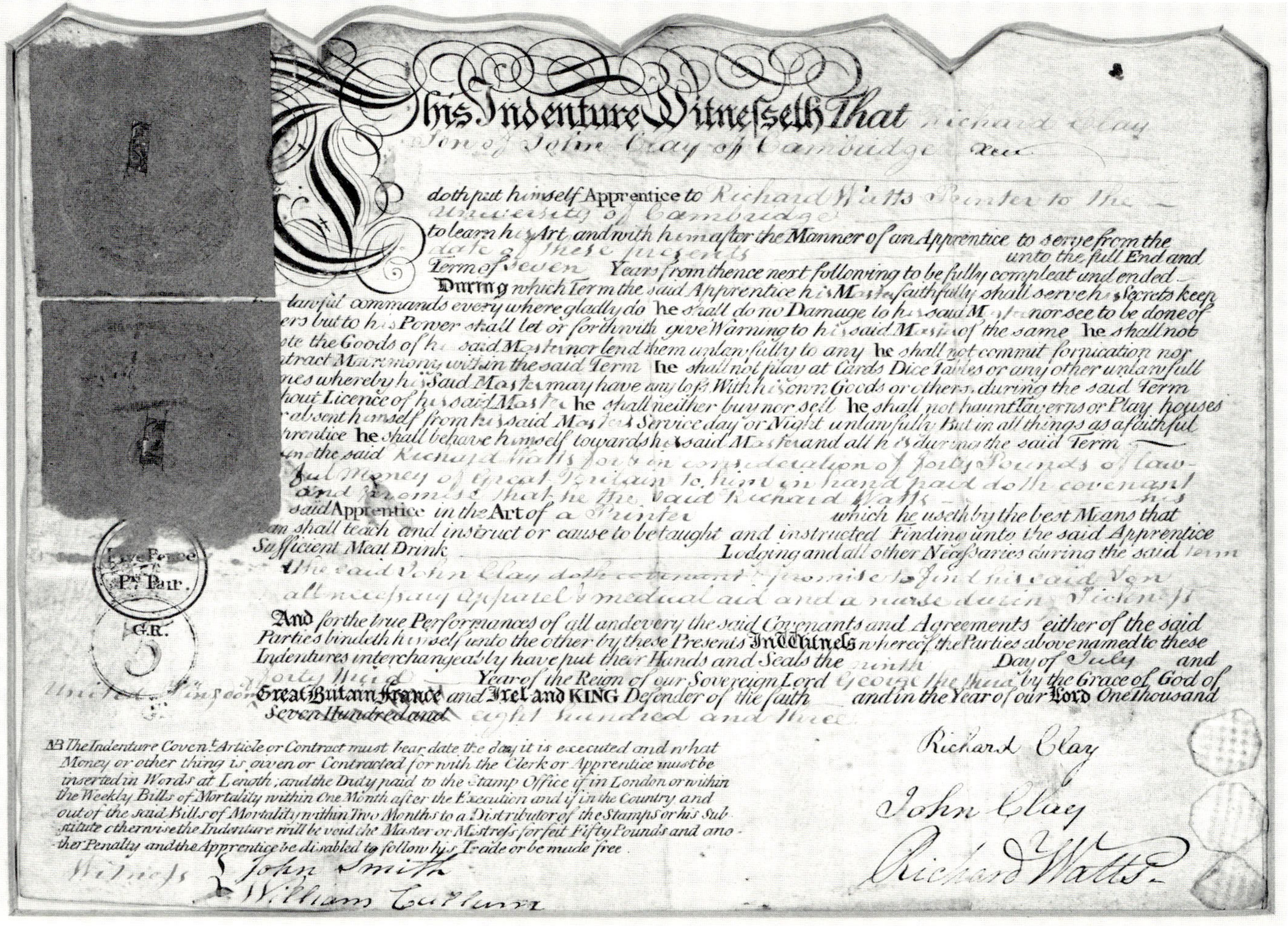

This Indenture Witnesseth That Richard Clay Son of John Clay of Cambridge &c

doth put himself Apprentice to Richard Watts Printer to the University of Cambridge to learn his Art and with him after the Manner of an Apprentice to serve from the date of these presents unto the full End and Term of Seven Years from thence next following to be fully compleat and ended During which Term the said Apprentice his Master faithfully shall serve his Secrets keep lawful commands every where gladly do he shall do no Damage to his said Master nor see to be done of ...ers but to his Power shall let or forthwith give Warning to his said Master of the same he shall not ...te the Goods of his said Master nor lend them unlawfully to any he shall not commit fornication nor ...tract Matrimony within the said Term he shall not play at Cards Dice Tables or any other unlawfull ...mes whereby his said Master may have any loss With his own Goods or others during the said Term ...hout Licence of his said Master he shall neither buy nor sell he shall not haunt Taverns or Play houses ...r absent himself from his said Master's Service day or Night unlawfully But in all things as a faithful ...prentice he shall behave himself towards his said Master and all his during the said Term ...n the said Richard Watts for & in consideration of Forty Pounds of lawful Money of Great Britain to him in hand paid doth covenant and promise that he the said Richard Watts his said Apprentice in the Art of a Printer which he useth by the best Means that ...n shall teach and instruct or cause to be taught and instructed Finding unto the said Apprentice Sufficient Meat Drink Lodging and all other Necessaries during the said term

the said John Clay doth covenant & promise to find his said Son all necessary apparel & medical aid and a nurse during sickness

And for the true Performances of all and every the said Covenants and Agreements either of the said Parties bindeth himself unto the other by these Presents In Witness whereof the Parties above named to these Indentures interchangeably have put their Hands and Seals the ninth Day of July and forty third Year of the Reign of our Sovereign Lord George the third by the Grace of God of United Kingdom Great Britain France and Ireland KING Defender of the faith and in the Year of our Lord One thousand Seven Hundred and eight hundred and three

NB The Indenture Covent Article or Contract must bear date the day it is executed and what Money or other thing is given or Contracted for with the Clerk or Apprentice must be inserted in Words at Length; and the Duty paid to the Stamp Office if in London or within the Weekly Bills of Mortality within One Month after the Execution and if in the Country and out of the said Bills of Mortality within Two Months to a Distributor of the Stamps or his Substitute otherwise the Indenture will be void the Master or Mistress forfeit Fifty Pounds and another Penalty and the Apprentice be disabled to follow his Trade or be made free

Witness John Smith
William Catlum

Richard Clay
John Clay
Richard Watts

Indenture of Richard Clay I signed in 1803

of the University and its suppliers. He might have been apprenticed to a local tradesman or perhaps taken up some non-academic appointment with one of the colleges, and ended his days either as a worthy local draper or a minor University official. Even a printing apprenticeship in 1803 might have led to nothing more than the life of a small provincial printer, except for the unusual developments at the University Press. Here it is desirable to outline the state of printing technique at the time – techniques which had hardly changed for 350 years.

Single pieces of type were composed in lines by hand in a 'stick', and then transferred, after proofing, on to a flat surface to be imposed in pages – being locked up in metal frames, known as chases. The resulting page-shaped printing surface was (and is) called a forme. One or more formes would be placed on the bed of a press, made of wood, for the actual printing. This was carried out by hand, the raised surface of the type being inked with dabbers, called ink balls. Paper was lowered on to the inked forme by means of devices known as tympan and frisket, and then the whole bed of the press was wound under a flat surface known as a platen. By pulling a bar and activating a screw the printer would bring down the platen and force the paper into contact with the forme, thus causing the ink to be transferred to the paper. The bed of the press was wound outwards and the printed sheet removed. This was of necessity a slow process owing to the limited size of the platen. Large sheets of paper had to be printed with two pulls – half the bed being wound in first and then followed by the second half.

Those who felt the techniques of printing should be improved were often outside the trade itself. Among printers and associated craftsmen there was a marked tendency to resist change, but given that change was desirable the requirement was three-fold. Firstly, the composition of type needed to be speeded up. This proved to be the most difficult of achievement as compositors firmly believed that traditional methods were best, and also because innovators tended to channel their energies in the wrong direction. Secondly, the printing press needed to be made more efficient. This was a more acceptable notion and some steps in this direction had been taken before the nineteenth century. Thirdly, in order to assist the mass production of printed matter it would be useful to devise some form of duplication of printing surfaces, which, additionally, would avoid the cost of resetting type for reprints of popular works.

There was always a danger that technical improvement would be premature, being devised in an unsympathetic industrial and social climate. Machines could be invented which were before their time because manufacturing techniques were not sufficiently advanced and, in any case, because there was not the reading public demanding printed matter in the quantities which would make the machines an economic proposition.

It was because Richard Clay and his immediate successors lived in that period of history when the expansion of industry enabled theoretical conceptions to be transformed into actual machines, and when political reform was creating new demands for reading matter, and because they were able to grasp these facts, that they emerged as major purveyors of the printed word.

The path was not straight; there were false starts and blind alleys, but various Clays, as will be noted, were willing to try any new technique if it appeared to help them in their work, and in that mysterious hereditary fashion most of them seemed to have a leaning towards mechanical invention themselves.

Richard Clay's genetical forebears have been mentioned. His technological forebears, if the phrase may be used, were a mixed bunch, the only shared characteristic being an inventive faculty.

The first method devised to speed up composition was by using logotypes – pieces of type on which two or more characters were cast – the theory being that a compositor would save time if he picked out parts of words from the case rather than individual letters. The value of this reform was more apparent than real, but it was pursued throughout the eighteenth and nineteenth centuries. In 1785 the idea received the support of John Walter, who having established the Logographic Printing Office to promote the system, founded *The Daily Universal Register* (later *The Times*) to publicise the publications of the Logographic Printing Office. Charles, third Earl Stanhope (1753–1816), an eccentric politician, was also attracted to logotypes and devised a new system together with special compositors' cases. Both Walter's and Stanhope's systems were doomed to failure because the number of case divisions increased for each added combination, producing cases of unmanageable size. The greater the number of logotypes the greater was the strain on the compositor's memory, and it was found quicker and simpler to set individual characters.

The next thought was to assemble pieces of type in channels and release them in the order required at the touch of a key. This was the basis of early composing machines, most of which proved to be economic failures. Difficulties arose over the distribution of type after use and over justification. Dirty type also tended to stick in the channels. By the 1880s all these drawbacks had been overcome in the monster Paige machine, but by this time the real solution had been discovered by Ottmar Mergenthaler (inventor of the Linotype) which consisted of the composition of matrixes rather than pieces of type and for the machine to combine both composing and casting. Before this point, however, Clays had interested themselves in a number of composing devices and machines.

Attempts had been made from an early date to improve the performance of the wooden press, mostly by adding metal parts, culminating in the press built by the Swiss typefounder, Wilhelm Haas, in 1772. This press, later improved by his son, had an iron frame. The new press with which, however, Richard Clay would have been familiar, was that invented by Lord Stanhope. This had an all-metal basis and while retaining the conventional screw was a great improvement on the wooden press because of the compound power provided by means of levers.

Duplication of printing surfaces dates back at least to 1700, when Johann Muller, a German Lutheran minister in Holland, invented the process of stereotyping. He was followed by others – including William Ged, an Edinburgh goldsmith, in 1725 and Firmin Didot in 1795. Lord Stanhope knew of the previous history of stereotyping but he purchased in 1800 the 1784 'invention' of Andrew Foulis, a Glasgow printer, 'for the purpose of giving it to the world at large'. He also claimed to have made improvements. He certainly carried out experiments in London and at his house at Chevening, Kent, where his chief stereotyper was Christopher Matthews (called 'Kit' by Stanhope in his notes).[3] Basically, the process consisted of making a mould of a page of type by pouring plaster of Paris over it, baking the mould and then casting duplicate plates from it. Stanhope's concern with stereotyping arose, among other things, from his interest in education (he founded schools for poor children) and the need for cheaper schoolbooks. He also wanted to improve the quality of printed books, as through constant use type became worn and books difficult to read.

During the tenure of office of University Printer at Cambridge by Richard Watts, young Clay's master, the University received an offer of the 'secret' of stereotype printing. The University was naturally interested in any process which would cheapen the production of Bibles and prayer books, for example, and despite an earlier unfortunate experience with Ged's invention in the 1730s, it was decided to investigate the offer. This was made not by Lord Stanhope (he refused to be involved in commercial proceedings), but by Andrew Wilson, the London printer employed by Stanhope. Agreement was reached and by 1809 a stereotype foundry had been built at Cambridge. So keen was Watts to publicise the process that when he printed the prospectus for the East India Company's new college at Haileybury in 1806 he caused the imprint to read: 'Stereotyped by Richard Watts, M.DCCC.VI.'

Continual financial disputes with Wilson and doubts as to whether the process was indeed so secret as was made out led to an eventual breakdown in the agreement. The governors of the University Press, the Syndics, were also not altogether happy in their relations with their Printer, Watts. In 1808 two of their number were appointed to examine the Press accounts as it was said that no profit had been made for five years. Irritated by the enquiry, Watts resigned on June 13th 1808, and at the next meeting of the Syndics his resignation was accepted. A subsequent application to withdraw his resignation 'in consequence of the more due consideration of the causes which led to it' was made to the Syndics, but they resolved that no answer could be given until the examination of the accounts was concluded, and apparently the matter was never reopened. The accounts were not finally completed until June 1809, when, Watts having surrendered his patent into the hands of the Vice-Chancellor, it was resolved that a new Printer be elected in October. Watts was paid £150 'for his attention to the Stereotype office to that period, in addition to the sums advanced to him on that account' and also £150 for his services as Printer from November 1808 to June 17th 1809.[4] By this time the apprenticeship of Richard Clay was nearing its end and he was 'turned over' to the new Printer, John Smith, for the remainder of the apprenticeship.[5] Under Smith the Press expanded, the number of presses in use increasing from eight in 1809 to thirteen in 1813.

The significance of the stereotyping episode as far as Richard Clay is concerned was that instead of being apprenticed in an unchanging atmosphere he was exposed at an early age to what were for the day advanced techniques. According to family tradition he went up to London to assist in Stanhope's experiments. This was not unlikely, as there was communication between Cambridge and Wilson's office, and one of the Cambridge apprentices, Macintosh, actually got a job with Wilson. In London Clay would have seen the Stanhope presses – two of which the University was subsequently to purchase and five of which were in the possession of Clays as late as 1887. He could also have met Christopher Matthews, Stanhope's stereotyper, and it is probably more than a coincidence that an Edward Matthews, who is mentioned in various works on Bungay[6] as a 'pupil of Earl Stanhope', was employed at the printing office of John Childs in Bungay. Richard Clay could have kept in touch with Matthews and come to know John Childs, an early printer of standard works and serial publications.

The Bungay firm had been founded by Richard Morris and Charles Brightly in 1798. It specialised in copperplate engravings, but Brightly was also one of the pioneer users of the stereotyping process and wrote a pamphlet on the subject in 1809.[7] In the same year John Childs joined him as a representative.

Trade flourished so much that Brightly bought the old town workhouse and converted it into a printing shop. Childs married

Brightly's daughter and in 1823 took over the firm, taking his sons, Robert and Charles into it as partners. It was known as John and R. Childs and later Childs & Son. John Childs died in 1853 and was succeeded by his son Charles.

Richard Clay began to use the stereotyping process himself in the 1820s and from the evidence of an account book of 1833 it is clear that the Childs family had some unspecified financial dealings with him. J. Childs was paying interest, and £100 represented 'balance of account'. C. Childs paid £300 cash, but for what it is not stated, and Robert Childs was paying interest on £1000. So that when Charles Childs died suddenly on December 26th 1876, it was not surprising that Clays took over the business in Bungay, with which they have been associated ever since. But if Richard Clay had not been involved in Stanhope's stereotyping experiments this might never have happened.

While Richard Clay was fortunate enough to have been apprenticed in what was an exciting technical atmosphere, nevertheless his prospects would have been limited if he had stayed in the provinces and so, in the same way as other apprentices who founded printing dynasties, he made his way to London, which for centuries had been the centre of Britain's printing trade.

NOTES

1. Now a college hostel.

2. An examination of Loggan's plan of Cambridge (1688) reproduced in *The University Printing Houses at Cambridge* (Cambridge, 1962) and a modern map of the City Centre will indicate the small compass of the area involved.

3. See *Charles Earl Stanhope and the Oxford University Press* by Horace Hart. New edition published by the Printing Historical Society, London, 1966.

4. Press Syndics Order, June 26th 1810.

5. Press Syndics Order, June 26th 1810: 'That the Apprentices be articled to the Printer and that, at the expiration of his office they be transferred to his Successor.'

6. *Old Bungay* by Ethel Mann (Heath Cranton Ltd, 1934); *Rayner's Bungay Almanack* 1891 (H. Rayner, Market Place, Bungay).

7. *Method of Casting Stereotypes as practised by Charles Brightly*. E. C. Bigmore and C. W. H. Wyman in *A Bibliography of Printing* (1886) comment: 'The author was a member of a firm of printers at Bungay, who were largely engaged in the production of popular literature at low cost. They were among the first to adopt stereotyping, and at some risk, for the printers of the day were violently opposed to what they regarded as exceedingly inimical to their interests. The system followed by Charles Brightly was that of Lord Stanhope, with some slight variations.' The firm was well known for its stereotyping work and craftsmen trained at Bungay were in demand. One Robert Smith, after being employed by Childs, travelled about teaching the process. He died in 1820, but his son, Thomas, emigrated to the United States and founded a leading family of printers and stereotypers. Laurence Johnson, the eminent Philadelphia typefounder (died 1860) had the opportunity of studying stereotyping at Bungay and was able to make use of this knowledge when he emigrated to the United States.

CHAPTER TWO

London

THE REASON WHY Richard Clay went to London is obvious. The metropolis was the place where an ambitious young man could get on, particularly in the printing trade. It has been a family tradition, repeated in various books, that he set up in business on his own in Devonshire Street, Bishopsgate, in 1817 (1816, or even 1815, according to some accounts). This is not entirely accurate. He became responsible for the printing side of an existing business in Devonshire Street in 1818 and gradually assumed greater control until he took it over completely in 1827.

It is owing to an Act of Parliament requiring the registration of printing presses, that it is possible to show that Richard Clay did not set up on his own on his arrival in London, but joined an existing firm. Three early account books (two ledgers and a cash book), preserved by the firm of Clays, are not exclusively Richard Clay's but belonged to the various successors of Burton and Briggs, stationers and booksellers, who added printing to their activities in 1816.

The circumstances which led to the registration of printing presses arose in 1799 when the Government was concerned with the growth of seditious organisations. By the Act of 39 George III, cap. 79, every person having a printing press or types for printing was required to sign a document to this effect, attested by one witness, and deliver it to the local Clerk of the Peace. Such declarations as still exist in County records are of a set form and do not give much information about the nature of the printing presses but they do constitute a reliable guide to the existence of firms or partnerships in the early part of the nineteenth century.

In Critchett and Woods' *Post Office Directory* for 1816, Burton and Briggs, Stationers and Booksellers, are listed as being at 156 Leadenhall Street. On July 30th 1816 Samuel Burton, John Allen and James Briggs of No. 9 Devonshire Street, Bishopsgate, declared to the Clerk of the Peace for the City of London, that they had three printing presses and types for printing on the premises. Their witness was John Smart Jun. of 156 Leadenhall Street (who, from the address, was probably an employee of the stationery firm). John Allen may have been a printer brought in when the two booksellers decided to expand their business into printing in premises a few streets away from their shop. By 1817 the new firm had acquired the name of Burton & Co., which is listed as 'printers and stationers' at 9 Devonshire Street in Johnstone's *Street Directory* of that year, Burton and Briggs, 'stationers', continuing at 156 Leadenhall Street.

By 1818, Samuel Burton is listed on his own as a stationer at the Leadenhall Street address (Critchett & Woods' *Directory*). What happened to Briggs is not known but by this time Burton must have come across the young Clay because on September 21st 1818 Samuel Burton (of Leadenhall Street), Richard Clay (of 9 Devonshire Street) and Samuel Smith of Bethel Place, Camberwell, made a declaration to the Clerk of the Peace that they had three presses and types for printing at No. 9 Devonshire Street, Bishopsgate. Their witness was James Forrest, of No. 14 Blossom Street, Norton Folgate (which is at the end of Bishopsgate). Smith is shown in directories as a 'Hardwareman' of 6 Norton Folgate.

It would be reasonable to assume that Burton had lost his partner Briggs and had obtained financial support from Smith, but that as both men had other concerns to run they needed a printer at the Devonshire Street premises. John Allen, as the early ledger shows, had gone off on his own, and so they took on Clay as the printer.

From Robson's *Directory* for 1819 it appears that Clay had been promoted to be a partner since 'Burton, Clay and Smith' are listed as printers at the Devonshire Street address, while 'Burton and Smith' continue to be listed as stationers and booksellers at the Leadenhall Street address. In the 1821 issue of Robson the firm is still called Burton, Clay and Smith but by 1823 (Piggot & Co.'s *Directory*) the name has been shortened to Burton and Clay.

Exactly when Clay joined the firm is not known but from the ledger it looks as if Allen had left some time in 1817 and the declaration shows that Clay was among those legally responsible for the printing presses from September 1818 onwards. There is no further declaration involving Clay in the Guildhall records until 1829 when he had clearly started his own business.

How he met Burton is also unknown but he was not without contacts in London. We know, for example, from an obituary in the *Printers' Register* of July 1st 1865, that a friend and fellow-apprentice, A. Macintosh, was in London at least by 1815. Since he had been apprenticed to John Burges, who held the office of University Printer at Cambridge from 1795–1802, Macintosh must have been older than Clay and as he went straight to London and had held several jobs before setting up on his own he would have been well established by the time Clay arrived. One of the jobs had been with Lord Stanhope's printer, Andrew Wilson, which argues close contact between the Cambridge apprentices and the Stanhope circle.

Also in London was Clay's old master, Richard Watts, who on leaving Cambridge had first gone to Broxbourne in Hertfordshire, where he stayed until 1815. While there he had been appointed Printer to the East India Company's College at Haileybury. This appointment he retained when he removed his press to London in 1816. So Clay could have sought him out at Crown Court, Temple Bar.

Whatever the case, Richard Clay received an appointment with Burton and moved to 9 Devonshire Street and lived on the premises. The early ledger provides evidence that he could not have possibly made a living out of the small returns from the firm, which was merely an extension of Burton's stationery business. As a stationer Burton had probably found that people came to him to have their cards and bill-heads printed, and after a time decided he might as well have his own printing establishment as put the work out to others.

One or more of the presses at Devonshire Street must have been a copperplate rolling press to print engraved cards, but unfortunately the certificates do not indicate what type of press is being registered and it is likely that only a few Parliamentarians, when considering the Act, would have realised that there were, in fact, different types of press. As an example of the vagueness of description, R. M. Jameson on August 23rd 1838 simply says he has a printing press, yet on a separate card attached to his declaration in the Guildhall records he advertises himself as a letterpress and copperplate printer.

While the printing of large plates and book illustrations needed some experience, the jobbing printing of trade and personal cards would be a fairly easy business to start up in. A passage in Tegg's *The Complete Book of Trades* (1842) reads: '. . . a small trade in copperplate printing may be commenced with a couple of presses, a man and a boy, with all the *et ceteras* of blankets, ink and fittings up, with two hundred pounds'. That Burton's were actual copperplate printers is shown by the account books. Much of the business was in cards and the amounts of money involved were so small that there would have been little point in accepting orders simply to put them out to another copperplate printer. Moreover, others in the printing trade sub-contracted orders for cards to Burton's.

There are several payments entered to E. B. Cross, engraver, for engraving and repairing plates. The initials may be an error as there was an engraver named Edward Harris Cross conveniently at 92 Leadenhall Street. It is reasonable to assume that the firm had no engraver on the staff but did carry out the printing. Other payments were made to 'Perkins', engraver, in the cash book.

The ledger in question is narrow (12½ inches long by 4 inches wide) and still carries the small engraved label 'Sold by Burton & Briggs, 156 Leadenhall Street, London'. The paper is watermarked 'J. Jellyman 1814' and a third of the roughly 400 pages have not been used. Each pair of pages bears a number and these run from 1 to 75, twenty-eight pages at the front being used for an Index. The first part covers the years 1816–19 and then there are five blank pages, when re-numbering begins at 100 in August 1824. Only fourteen pages are used until 1826, and the rest of the book is blank.

The first customer (June 7th 1816) was R. Iveson of the 'Three Tuns', Aldgate, who had 1000 tickets printed for 12*s*. He followed this with an order for six large bills on July 26th at 9*s.* and another 1000 tickets at 12*s.* on October 24th, paying by cash in December. The orders for cards often came from other printers or from printing trade workers who were obviously doing a little 'print farming'. While John Price is designated 'Printer', 'Forest' and 'Fowler' are noted as 'compositors', Cave as 'Pressman' and Pounceby as 'binder'. Their accounts are very small. White, the printer of New Street, on the other hand, ordered labels, bills, 'law cases' to the tune of £8. 16*s.* 9*d.* in 1816 and another printer, James Smith, had 150 octavo page songs printed for 6*s.* (for which he apparently never paid). Samuel Burton himself fed more substantial work into the firm – mostly for cards, labels and way bills during 1817–18 to the value of £90, the biggest item (£29. 5*s.* 6*d.*) being for the 'Vaccine Establ.' (presumably labels).

There are few entries on the Purchase side, one of which, however, is for John Clark, Old Bethlem, who repaired two chases for 5*s.* 6*d.* and provided 'new joint for stove' for 4*s.* 6*d.* in 1818, and another which is puzzling. Charles Clay supplied in 1817 'ornamental rules', 'Furniture 10 line' and 'Fount of 8 line Ros.' at a total cost of £2. 16*s.* 6*d.* This may have been Richard Clay's brother, born in 1798. According to Mary Aimée Clay he worked for a bookseller in Huntingdon and then went to London where he was employed by 'Baldwin & Co.' in the City. He died in 1821. There is certainly a Thomas Lovell of Huntingdon who bought two lots of 100 black edged cards at 5*s.* a time from the firm in 1818, the account being 'settled by S.B.' which might indicate some connection between the Clays and Burton, but what Charles was doing selling composing material can only be conjectured. Perhaps his brother was doing him a good turn. Henry Marshall, of Cambridge, who ordered bills and cards and paid 15*s.* for the repair of a plate, was a friend of Charles Clay, according to Mary Aimée Clay.

While 'John Allen' is a fairly common name it can be surmised that this entry referred to the former partner-printer. In 1817 he ordered at various times 'bills', 'tracts' and 'letters' to the value of £3. 1*s.* 6*d.*, which indicates that he had set up as a stationer on his own.

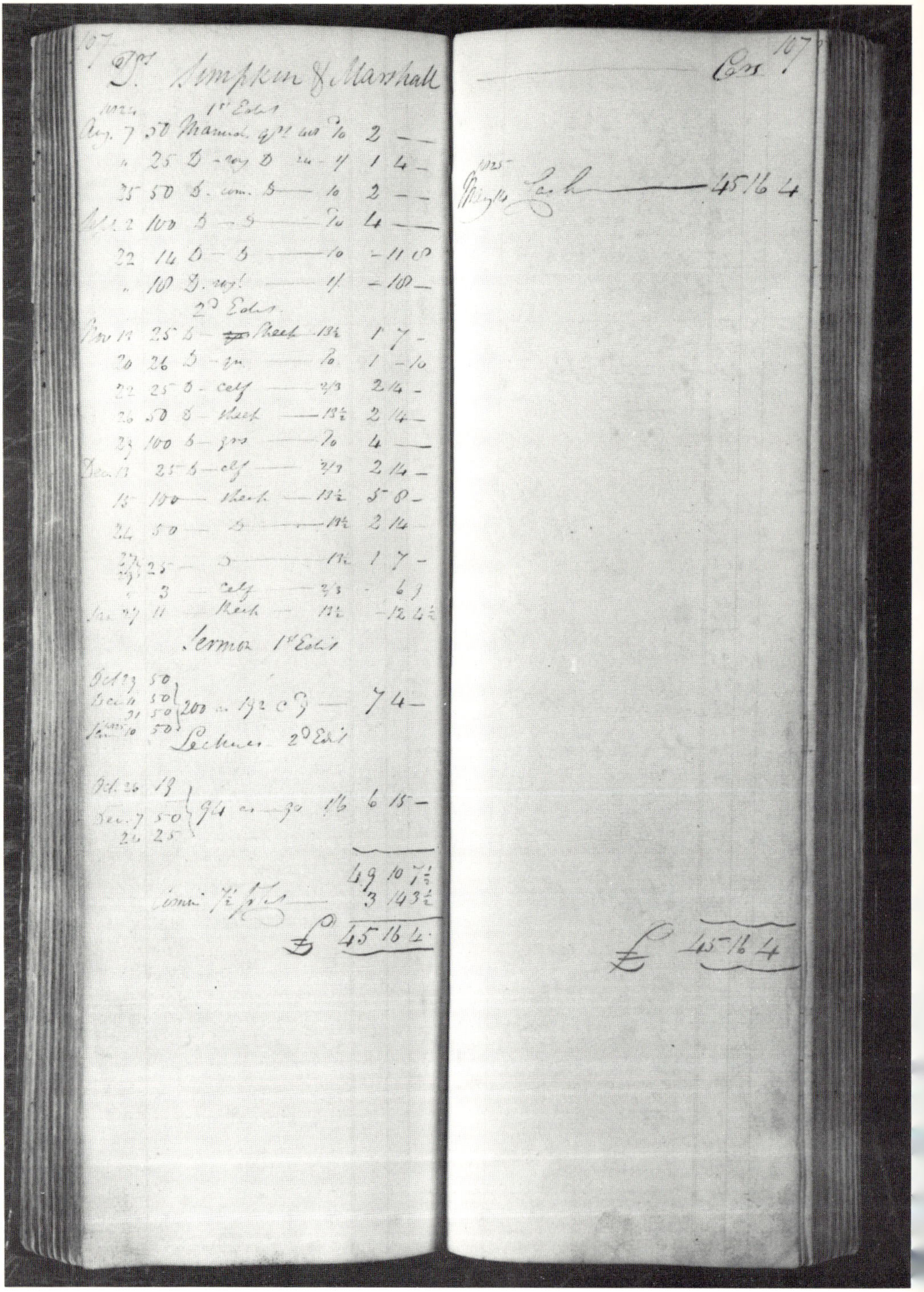

The account book of 1816 showing the page for Simpkin & Marshall

Why the modest little ledger should have been used again after an interval of five years when, in fact, in 1819 a large, professionally kept ledger had been started it is difficult to say – except that it may indicate a parting of the ways between Burton and Clay, who, as will be seen, began to use his own name as an imprint before actually leaving Devonshire Street.

The customers of 1824 and after in the small book include such well-known bookselling and publishing names as Rivington, Simpkin and Marshall and John Murray but the entries and the sums of money involved do not give the appearance of printing work. Fifty 'manuals' in sheep for £2 or 3 in calf for 6*s.* 9*d.* sound like account books: 25 'sermons' at 10*s.* or 25 'lectures' at £1. 16*s.* 0*d.* were probably pamphlets and part of the bookselling business.

In the later much more dignified ledger, with each customer's name written in copperplate script, Rivington, Simpkin and Marshall and John Murray do not appear (perhaps they were Burton's customers) but there are signs that printing for publishers, particularly for George Virtue, had begun. But in sheer weight of numbers the stationery sales predominate, followed by small jobbing printing, which apart from the inevitable cards, included work for publishers – 'wrappers', 'catalogues' and 'advertisements'.

This large ledger was not supplied by Burton but by Henry Harrison, stationer of 41 Bedford Street, Covent Garden. The reason is obvious – a large contra business was carried on with Mr Harrison, who numbered the Duchess of St Albans, Coutts bank, the Society of Arts, the Veterinary College and the Bank of Scotland among his customers. He sometimes paid in cash but more often in goods (paper, slate pencils, pens, receipt books and writing ink).

Burton and Clay's customers ranged from the Society of Guardians to the Horse Bazaar. The first required summonses, circulars and lists of members. The second was always a regular customer for catalogues for the sale of horses and carriages. Estate agents were supplied not only with posters but reams of paper as well. Apothecaries ordered labels for everything from lavender water to 'pectoral pills'.

The most revealing aspect of the ledger is, however, the information which shows that Burton and Clay gradually became what, for its day, was a large-scale stereotyping 'trade house'. Much of the work was concerned with making stereotype plates of book pages. Sometimes the composition was also carried out by the firm but rarely the actual printing. This was a period when the first signs of mass production publishing were visible and the stereotyping process was invaluable to those entrepreneurs who wanted to cut the cost of production of the small and somewhat crude books which were being issued to the growing reading public. Clay, and not Burton, would be responsible for this extension of business as the result of his earlier experiences, and it may well have occurred to him that he could escape from the narrow and not very profitable circumstances of a 'card' printer into book and periodical production and become a much more substantial figure in the trade. While, no doubt, the stereotyping of plates from which others would print showed a profit, nevertheless as a trained printer he would want to be responsible for whole jobs. It was not until 1825, however, that Virtue, for example, gave him such a complete job. The entry in the account book is as follows:

Account of Wedding Ring

Copy 30 nos	31. 10. 0.
Comp. & casting	139. 10. 0.
Press work 162,000	73. 17. 6.
coppers	18. 5. 6.
9,100 Printing 1/3	5. 9. 9.
Paper for do (1 rm from GV)	2. 3. 6.
Stitching 21,612	4. 17. 0.
Paper for No. 1 Wrap. 2 rm	2. 12. 0.
25 Wrap paper 15/-*d.*	18. 15. 0.
Casting wrap	2. 0. 0.
do advertisement	2. 14. 0.
Working 2,6000 do.	2. 10. 0.
5½ Rm Paper for do	5. 10. 0.
51500 Wrappers	5. 12. 6.
	£313. 6. 9*d.*

This was the biggest single order from Virtue, whose whole account in 1821 had amounted to no more than £34. 17*s*. 3*d*. Other publisher customers included Thomas Kelly, an early technical specialist, who published books on the steam engine, and James Shalders who ordered 500 pamphlets:

'Observations on Negro Slavery' —

7½ sheets demy 8vo £2. 4.	16. 10. 0*d*.
Corrections &c	19. 0*d*.
Stitching	11. 3.
Cold Pressing	7. 6.
Paid carriage & postage	8. 6.
	£18. 16. 3*d*.

By 1828 Richard Clay was also printing (or possibly part-printing) a periodical entitled *The Theatre* ('composing 13 pages, No. 14 . . . £2. 14. 0*d*.').

The purchase side of the ledger also provides a clue to the expansion of the business. In 1820 only £4. 16*s*. 0*d*. worth of printing ink was bought – from V. Griffiths and this was paid for in kind ('bills of parcel' and 'letters'). The year before, ink had been purchased from Fourdrinier Hunt & Co., paper merchants, to the value of only £1. 7*s*. 0*d*. The firm may have continued to make its own ink as well, as printing ink making as a separate industrial function was then in its infancy. But by 1828 the firm was buying ink from Ben Smith, Shacklewell, to the value of £19. 5*s*. 0*d*. and for the next year £20. 10*s*. 0*d*. Vaughan Griffiths was a well-known early printing ink manufacturer and there is a suggestion that Ben Smith took over his business. Paper was purchased from such firms as Fourdrinier Hunt & Co. (the £41. 10*s*. 2*d*. in 1819 included the supply of printing ink) but by 1829 this firm had changed its name to Hunt Fourdrinier and in that year the purchases had mounted to £124. 17*s*. 9*d*. and in the next year to £313. 11*s*. 0*d*.

Where Clay got his plaster of Paris before stereotyping in a big way is not noted, but from 1828 he began dealing with J. D. Smith, a supplier. In the two years 1828 and 1829 he bought 64 cwts., always in lots of 1 cwt. at 7*s*. a time until September 1829 when 13 cwts. were bought at one go and another 14 cwts. in the October. This was when Clay was launching himself independently.

Type was purchased from well-known typefounders. The bill from W. Thorowgood in 1828 amounted to only £14. 13*s*. 11*d*. The next year it dropped to £6. 10*s*. 1*d*. but in 1830 it had risen to £45. 2*s*. 0*d*. This included the major item of '267 lb. English No. 3 Roman' at £24. 9*s*. 6*d*. During the three years Clay bought various quantities of Long Primer Open Black, Great Primer Script, Brevier, Bourgeois, 'Pearl fractions' and Small Pica. The bill from Vincent Figgins in 1828 amounted to £5. 6*s*. 2*d*. for one item only – 70 lb. 12 ozs. Canon. Nothing was bought in 1829 but in 1830 the total sum involved was £23. 4*s*. 4*d*. for Small Pica, 2-line Brevier, English and the major item, 105 lb. in all, of Brevier at £23. 4*s*. 4*d*.

Two other sets of entries show that Clay had absorbed new technical ideas. The first is that concerned with Edmund Fry, the typefounder, with whom Clay did a contra business. What goods Fry supplied is not known, but they were presumably founts of type because Clay sold him back old metal. Clay not only printed Fry's circulars but also produced for him metal ornaments or polytypes. Today such blocks would be photographed from original drawings and produced by photo-engraving with duplicates by electrotyping, but at that time illustrations for letterpress printing were produced from wood engravings. The multiplication of engravings by stereotyping them in hard metal would reduce the cost of commonly used illustrations such as the Royal Arms. We find therefore that Clay cast for Fry such items as 'Indenture', 'King's Arms', 'London' (presumably the arms of the City), 'Eagle and Serpent', 'Eagle', 'Sun' and 'Ornamental Magna Charter' [*sic*]. Clay did a small trade in supplying these stock blocks to other customers. Milne and Duckworth had 17 casts of the King's Arms in 1826 at prices ranging from 1*s*. 3*d*. to 2*s*. 3*d*. each. Harjette & Saville also had casts of the King's Arms and various ornaments. 'Simmonds' went in for his own designs.

The other entry relates to Robert Harrild, founder of the business which flourished under that name. Here it is necessary to refer to another limiting factor in early printing – the method of applying the ink to the forme of type. For hundreds of years this had been carried out by the use of ink balls. An ink ball consisted of wooden stock and a piece of leather stuffed with wool or hair. The balls were inked and then moved in a circular motion across the forme in such a way that smearing did not take place. This dexterous operation was called 'beating the forme'. Their cleaning was a very smelly business.[1] The use of ink balls persisted until the 1820s but the invention of the printing machine meant that rollers had become an economic necessity. Various coverings such as leather were tried out on rollers but these were unsuccessful. More successful was the manufacture from a composition of glue and molasses. There is a division of opinion as to who was the actual inventor of composition rollers and ink balls, but R. Harrild & Co. were responsible for breaking down the resistance to this new form of inking and for the sales efforts necessary. By 1819 Harrild's were advertising a composition roller which would be kept in complete repair for 6*s*. a quarter. Clay took advantage of this offer and in the ledger there is recorded in 1819: '12 months quarterage for 4 rollers at 6/-*d*.' and '12 months quarterage for 1 ball at 9/-*d*.'. This could indicate that Clay had four metal presses and one wooden press at that date but we cannot be sure that one or more rollers might not be kept in reserve. He had banished, however, the evil-smelling leather ink ball from his works.

Richard Clay continued conscientiously to supply the usual 100 cards at ten shillings for Mrs Coutts, the 200 'tea papers' at 2*s*. 6*d*. for George Phillips, the grocer, and the 500 Seidlitz powder labels[2] at 10*s*. to David Grant through the firm of Burton and Clay, but he had discovered that there was a bigger world to conquer. While Clay eventually took the whole business over in 1827 there is evidence that as early as 1824 he had acted as an independent printer. What the arrangements were with Burton it is hard to say, but in April 1824 Clay took over the printing of a quarterly periodical called *The Herald of Peace* from B. Bensley, of Bolt Court, Fleet Street, who had been printing it for the publishers, Hamilton and Adams, since 1819. The imprint from the second quarter of 1824 and to the Index of the whole yearly volume is 'R. Clay, Printer, 9 Devonshire Street, Bishopsgate'.

Clay found himself in the position which sometimes arises in the best of firms. While he was no doubt grateful to Burton for giving him the initial chance and for the backing he had received, nevertheless the firm had expanded as the result of his endeavours and specialist knowledge. As with others before and since, he felt the time had come to use his skill and knowledge more directly for himself. The death or retirement of Burton provided the opportunity of formalising the position.

NOTES

1. For a description see *A History of Printing Ink, Balls and Rollers* by Colin Bloy (Wynkyn de Worde Society, London, 1966).

2. Illustrations of these labels appear on p. 52 of *Packaging and Print* by Alec Davies.

CHAPTER THREE

Bread Street Hill

RICHARD CLAY HAD advanced both technically and in the range of business and, at some point, he took over the firm in Devonshire Street completely. A study of the not particularly reliable street directories of the day suggests this took place in 1827. The directories reveal that Samuel Burton kept his stationery business going at 156 Leadenhall Street until 1827; then in 1828 the address was taken over by 'Fauntleroy and Burton jun.', stationers. The inference is that Burton senior had either died or retired in 1827, for also in that year 'Burton, Clay & Smith' printers disappear from the directories and 'Wm' Clay is noted at 9 Devonshire Street in Kent's *Directory*. It is too much of a coincidence to imagine that another printer with the same surname had set up at the same address, and the 'Wm' must therefore be a misprint (in Critchett's *Directory* of 1829 the correct name, Richard Clay, is given as at the Devonshire Street address).

George A. Ferguson 'accredited commissioner' of the *British and Colonial Printer & Stationer* visited Clays' works in 1906 and, in the course of an article in his journal, stated: 'The foundation of the House of Clay may be said to date back to about the year 1827.' This coincides with the evidence of the directories and with inferences from entries in an old surviving cash book, dated 1826–9. From 1826 onwards various relatives of Richard Clay, including his father, John, his brother, Percival, the merchant, and his mother-in-law, Mrs Painter, paid in sums of money, to be repaid later. It is unlikely that these loans would have been necessary if the partnership with Burton and Smith had continued in being. Moreover, entries also show that Richard Clay disposed of some stock to raise money. It is clear that he had taken over as sole proprietor.

Under his control the business expanded. The wage bills, indicating the number employed, rose gradually each year. During 1826 and 1827, however, they sometimes fell to only £7 a week. This was because the trade was still suffering from the slump of 1825, when a large number of banks had failed. Recovery came in 1828 when the weekly wage bill never fell below £11 and sometimes reached nearly £40. In 1829 there are frequent entries of £50 or more. The difficulties of the period had led two brothers, George and Charles Seares, both pressmen employed by John King of College Hill, to propose the foundation of a Printers Pension Society. At a meeting in the King's Head Tavern, Poultry, on December 3rd 1828, the Society was formally established, and Richard Clay subscribed £1 on December 21st. Presumably subscriptions were due each January for his next subscription (again for £1) is dated January 20th 1829.

The increase in work necessitated a bigger building and here we have precise evidence from the cash book of Clay's moves. It is in this book that the name of 'Taylor', a printer, first appears. He was later to be a Clay partner. On August 26th 1826 there is a cash entry: 'Taylor (Printing for Beadle) . . . £3. 0. *6d.*' and later, on December 20th 1828 on the other side of the cash book: 'Taylor (cards Philpot) £1. 8. *0d.*' indicating that a small amount of work passed from one printer to the other. From other entries it seems that Taylor abandoned his own business to look after the transfer of Clay's works to Bread Street Hill. But before this event the gradual increase in work, as shown by the wages bill, had led to the taking over of additional but temporary premises. For a short time Clay rented extra space in Warwick Square. On March 9th 1829 for the first time 'Wages and Sundries (£29. 16. *9d*)' carries an additional note: 'Dev. St.' and underneath there is another entry: 'Wages Warwick Square £44. 18. *6d.*' Entries for wages and sundries for both establishments continued until September 26th. On July 21st Clay had paid the British Fire Office £10. *2s. 6d.* in respect to Warwick Square, presumably for fire insurance, and on October 19th paid 'Hinton' £23 rent for these premises. This indicates that taking the premises was a temporary expedient while a new works was being prepared at Bread Street Hill. On August 15th Taylor made another appearance in the cash book but with 'Bread Street Hill' in brackets. The sum concerned was £30 and similar entries occur in succeeding weeks, the amounts varying from £10 to £40. Taylor was clearly in charge of the new premises, which neared completion in September. 'Plaisterers' at Bread Street Hill received five shillings on September 5th and thereafter the entries tell their own story: 'September 12: sundry expenses in removing 10*s.* 11*d.*'; 'September 26: Public House (Bill) Removing . . . 4/2'; 'October 3: Steadman for Vans from Dev. St. £2. 9. 0*d.*'; 'October 12 – Clock for Composing Room'; 'November 24 – "Van from Warwick Square" – £1. 14. 0*d.*'

The proprietors of the directories may be excused on this occasion if they failed to list Richard Clay as at Bread Street Hill until their 1831 editions. The letter carriers (who did the canvassing) probably found him still at Devonshire Street in late 1829 and entered their returns for the 1830 editions as such.

Clay had, however, made his declaration on October 12th 1829 to the Clerk of the Peace for the City that he had a printing press and types at 7 Bread Street Hill. This was witnessed by William Blott of that address. He received £1 from Clay on December 16th (cash book entry).

According to Robson's *Directory* for 1830 the occupants of 6 and 7 Bread Street Hill were Sykes Byall & Co., tobacco and snuff manufacturers, and William Davidson, wholesale stationer. Davidson is recorded at Dowgate Wharf in 1831 and it is obvious that Richard Clay took over his premises in the autumn of 1829 and it took a year for the directories to catch up with the change.

Robson's *Directory* of 1837 records that Clay was at both 7 and 8 Bread Street Hill together with 'Seckerson, silk manufacturer'. Since Clay printed this directory it is unlikely that he would make a mistake about his own premises. By the 1840 edition (also printed by Clay) Seckerson had disappeared. On April 24th 1839 Richard Clay made another declaration to the Clerk of the Peace declaring that he had printing presses (in the plural) and types for printing, so that in ten years the business had expanded sufficiently to take over extra premises and to add to the number of presses. During the years which followed adjoining space was taken over and by the time that George Ferguson wrote his article in 1906 he was able to refer to Clay's premises in Bread Street Hill as 'an imposing block of industrial buildings'.

Before leaving the old cash book (which was supplied by G. Roake, Stationer of 31 Strand) reference may be made to a few entries which additionally reveal something of the nature of the early Clay business. Ancillary work was not carried out on the premises – various payments were made to binders (Gray, Harley, Hunt & Leighton), and while the *Herald of Peace* was printed at Devonshire Street, an outsider, L. M. Stynes (who occasionally signed for his money) was responsible for the stitching. 'Young' also did some stitching for, among other things, a peace tract. Goods were bought from Roake, the stationer, including a diary. One entry is for J. Clarke 'Hotpresser'[1] and others are for Bonner, a wood engraver, and Jacob 'bill sticker'. Items purchased such as shooting sticks, press points, tympans and parchment refer to compositor's implements and attachments to the press. Type was bought either from typefounders such as Figgins or at auction sales. From 'Cope's Execrs.'[2] what appears to be an Albion press was bought in August 1828 for £28.

Indentures for an apprentice, James Robert Hart, cost £2. 17*s*. 0*d*. in January 1829 and in April those for Thomas Harper Bodley, Henry Carpenter and Chas. Collier cost £3. 3*s*. 0*d*. with an additional item 'Expenses of binding' of £5. 3*s*. 6*d*., so the total cost for each apprentice must have been about the same. Richard Clay appeared to have adhered to the old custom of the master printer contributing towards chapel festivities. When apprentices became journeymen there was usually a drinking function, and on April 21st 1829 he contributed £1 to 'T. Allen's (out of his time)' and on November 28th of the same year he gave £8. 1*s*. 4*d*. to the 'companionship' and 7*s* to the apprentice Hart. He also paid his share of each annual entertainment known as the 'Wayzgoose'[3] even if like many others he had his own spelling. He sometimes got let in for more than he had bargained. The 'weigh goose' in 1826 cost him £2. 1*s*. 0*d*.; in 1827 the entry is 'Weygoose (to clear bill) £1. 10. 0*d*.'

The premises at Bread Street Hill

and in 1828 it cost him £5 with '£3 ext. for friends' (whose friends is not indicated). In 1829 he promised £10 but it finally cost him £15, with 4*s.* 6*d.* additional expenses. In this year when he was contemplating the move to bigger premises the staff had obviously increased greatly in size, and so the bill was proportionately bigger.

The cash book shows that customers included such firms as Longman, Rees (later Longman & Co.). The Peace Society paid a regular £50 or so, presumably for *The Herald of Peace*. The Revd. G. C. Smith had a magazine called *The New Sailor* printed, and there are many entries for beadles and bellmen (minor ward officials) and for churches. Dealings with other printers may be noted. De la Rue & Co. did some work to the tune of £3. 17*s.* 6*d.*; Thompson (printer) for £3. 6*s.* 0*d.* and there are also the entries for Taylor. Surprising are the comparatively large sums involved in trade with Stephen Austin & Son, of Hertford, ranging from £34. 13*s.* 0*d.* to £131. 10*s.* 0*d.*, in four lots, from 1826–9.

Against the item for August 26th 1828 ('on account £50') is the notation 'T.L.' – perhaps Trade Ledger. Some of the entries in the cash book are easily interpreted but what can one make of, for instance, 'Lady Farnham and compositors . . . £1. 5. 0*d.*'?

The cash book ends in 1829, although a few entries have been made for January 1830 after 'Bankers Clerks Xs. Presents . . . £2.', but these have been crossed out, balances being carried forward to 'New Book' – a new regime was to begin at Bread Street Hill.

When Richard Clay first went there Bread Street Hill was a continuation of Bread Street, which led from Cheapside to Fish Street and Trinity Lane. Bread Street Hill then continued down to Upper Thames Street. The area around the hill was bombed during the 1939–45 war and only a vestigial remainder was left by 1964, and that is now built over. But even in Clay's time the area was considerably altered by the construction of Queen Victoria Street in the 1860s, which wiped Fish Street and Trinity Lane off the map.

In the ten years between the two statutory declarations the business had acquired a sufficiently sound economic basis to enable Richard Clay to abandon the old idea of living above the shop, and he moved to 5 Newmarket Terrace, Cambridge Heath. This is noted in the 1839 declaration, which was witnessed by his father, John Clay. It had not been until 1825, at the comparatively late age of 36, that Richard Clay had married 32-year-old Susanna Gregory Painter at the Parish Church of St Mary, Ely. Both from Cambridge, they knew each other when young and had been engaged for a time. The engagement was broken off because of lack of means, and not until Richard had found his feet economically did they agree to marry. The couple lived at 9 Devonshire Street and then Bread Street Hill before moving to Cambridge Heath. In 1845 they moved to 20 Park Terrace, Highbury, and finally to Avenue House, Muswell Hill, Hornsey, in 1847. Of their ten children four died in infancy. The eldest son was Charles John Clay, born July 2nd 1827. At eight years of age he went to St Paul's School, becoming captain of the school in 1845. Late in 1846 he entered Trinity College, Cambridge, graduating in 1850. He apparently thought of ordination and read theology for a time. Failing to get a fellowship at Sidney Sussex College, he decided to relinquish the idea of a University career and returned to London to learn the art of printing in his father's business. His two brothers, Richard and Arthur Lloyd, were born in 1839 and 1840 respectively. Both attended Highgate School, from which Richard entered the business, being technically apprenticed to his older brother, Charles John. Arthur joined the Indian Civil Service, from which he retired in 1890. He had initially entered his father's business as well but pleaded successfully to be allowed to enter for the Civil Service.[4] On retirement he was briefly a director of the family firm and died in 1903. The descendants of Charles John, who was appointed Cambridge University Printer, tended to be known as the 'Cambridge' Clays and those of Richard tended to concentrate on the business in London and Bungay, although the 'Cambridge' Clays were also concerned with the family firm as well. An early publishing customer was the firm of Macmillan, and in *The House of Macmillan* (1943) the author, Charles Morgan, makes reference to the production of the *Globe Shakespeare*, when Alexander Macmillan is quoted as writing of 'Clay, our printer'. This allusion is indexed under 'Clay, Richard' but in fact the *Globe Shakespeare* was printed by C. J. Clay at the University Press.

Mackie's steam type-composing machine

Old John Clay lived with his son's family, and just before he died he prevailed on his printer-son to publish some of his verses. The preface to the work, which is entitled *Elegies and Miscellaneous Pieces*, show Richard Clay's humanity and common sense. He obviously thought little of the merit of the poems, the titles of which indicate their contents – 'An Elegy on the Murder of Louis XVI', 'On the Death of George III', 'On the Death of Mary Ann Clay'; 'An Elegy on the lamented death of Miss M. Marshall' and 'On the Death of Mr Alderman Spencer'. The only relief from death is 'On a Robin – which built its nest in a water-pot in Mr Alderman Spencer's Garden in Cambridge'. The preface reads: 'The following pages, chiefly from the pen of our revered parent, were, after much, solicitation, passing through the Press, and for that purpose had been finally perused by him only a few days before his sudden departure on the 17th of February 1841. Being intended only as a memorial to those of his relatives and friends who knew, and would desire to cherish the recollection of his many virtues, it is unnecessary to speak of them as compositions. They will be valued from a far higher consideration . . .' At the end of the small book of 48 pages is a memorial to Charles Owen Clay.

Stereotyping remained an important aspect of the business and from a ledger of 1833 it is clear that plates for famous works were cast by Clays ('Gibbons' Rome'; 'Cruden's Concordance'). *Cruden's* was printed by Childs of Bungay, so that some of their work must have been sub-contracted to Clays. Among the bigger customers were Holdsworth and Ball ('Lardner's works'), Thomas Huntsman (religious works) and the Religious Tract Society (which became Lutterworth Press), for which special pages were stereotyped. The relation with Childs must have been close – Edward Hickman 'with J. R. & C. Childs' was paid for revising work. Under Longman & Co. in May 1833 there appears a printing charge for 'Hosland's works':

Printing 250 Patience	£3. 2. *6d.*
do 250 Decision	2. 17. *6d.*
Making ready	1. 4. o*d.*
	£7. 4. o*d.*

Much of the work was of a religious nature – Watt's Psalms, Henry's Bible, Cunningham's Hymns and Miss Harrison's Hymns, but there is occasional light relief. In July 1833 under 'Edward Lacey' the following appears:

Composing and casting Comic Annual . . .	20. 16. 0.
Printing 2000	30. 8. 0.
	£51. 4. 0*d*.

Mr Lacey was a good payer, his bill being settled in six months. His *Comic Annual* must have gone well, for he ordered another 2000 copies in February 1834 and a further similar quantity in the April of that year. In March 1835 his woodcuts and the stereotype plates were returned to him in two boxes.

There were some dealings with William Lenny, another printer. Clay sold him a press for £60 in May 1833, which he paid for in November 1834. He was not allowed to get away with that, being charged £7. 10*s*. 0*d*. for eighteen months' hire. This may be an example of a successful printer getting rid of an old wooden press, which had been replaced by the more up to date all-metal hand press, to a smaller tradesman. Lenny also bought cards, stereotype plates, paper and ink from Clay during 1833 and 1834, completing his payment by May 1836.

Caslon and Catherwood were added to the suppliers of type who continued to include William Thorowgood and Vincent Figgins. On the other hand there are indications that the firm cast some of its own type[5] since lead was bought from a variety of people, including 'Stranger' for £38. 13*s*. 3*d*. in 1833 and £79. 3*s*. 9*d*. in 1834. Antimony (the hardening element in type casting) was purchased from Hallett & Co. and from Thorowgood. Johnson, Mann & Co. supplied 'pearl Ashes',[6] oil and glue; and paper came from Jones & Brown, C. Burgess, John Dickinson & Co. and Smith & Chapman.

As the firm grew in size and importance Richard Clay achieved prominence in his own trade. By 1839 he was employing no less than 26 journeyman compositors and 14 apprentices. This was nothing like so many as, say, the two Hansards (53 men, 5 boys and 41 men and one boy respectively), but they had House of Commons work demanding a large attendance of compositors. The figure compared favourably with, say, Unwin's 5 men and 4 boys. By 1866 when the Children's Employment Commission reported on Printers and Stationers, Clays were stated as having 218 employees, compared with the 568 of Clowes and the 450 of Spottiswoodes.

An early association of printers had become inactive by 1816 but by 1835 there were proposals that it should be re-formed. Accordingly, a meeting was held at Stationers Hall on December 8th 1836 and Richard Clay was elected to the committee of the re-established Association of Master Printers, which is some indication of his standing, as the other members included some of the most influential men in the trade. Richard Clay thus became one of the signatories to the 1847 Compositors' Scale.

Not only did Richard Clay stand high in the estimation of his fellow master printers – he was also becoming one of the key printers to whom London's publishers could turn for first-class work. Some consideration should now be given to book production at Bread Street Hill.

NOTES

1. According to an advertisement in 1877 Clays had bought 'Gill's Patent Hot Rolling Machine' from Furnival & Co. By means of this machine printed sheets could be dried and pressed. The University Press, Cambridge, had one too.

2. See *The Albion Press* by Reynolds Stone, *Journal of the Printing Historical Society* No. 2, 1966. The press was manufactured by R. W. Cope by perhaps 1822. It is not certain when Cope died but if Clay bought a press from his executors in 1828 it must have been before that date.

3. Waygoose or wayzgoose – entertainment given by the master printer to mark the beginning of the season of working by candlelight. Later an outing and dinner.

4. In a letter, dated April 14th 1863 to Sir G. O. Trevelyan (then in India) the publisher, Alexander Macmillan wrote: 'If you come across a young man by name Arthur Clay – I think he is worth notice. He is a fine, modest, manly fellow, with lots of latent and admirable sense, not so able perhaps as Stigant or Stephenson, but likely to be much more practically useful. I shall be surprised if he does not prove to have great administrative power. I have known him for some years. His father is the great London printer, and tried to get him to take up with his own business; but his leanings were always to a more enterprising life. The wise, quiet and modest way in which he brought his father round to take his own view of what was best for him was really fine. There was not the least disobedience or kicking off the traces. He worked well at the business while he was at it, and only left off with his father's consent.' *Letters of Alexander Macmillan*, printed for private circulation 1908.

5. This is confirmed by the schedule of plant made in 1887 for the new limited company which took over the following year. Type-casting plant included three letter-casting machines as well as three hand moulds, letter-punches and matrices.

6. Used to make lye for cleaning formes of type.

CHAPTER FOUR

Victorian Book Production

AN EARLY PUBLISHER-CUSTOMER was the firm of Houlston and Stoneman, of 65 Paternoster Row, who were responsible for a wide range of 'interesting and instructive works'. Many of these were of a sentimental nature. *A Whisper to a Newly Married Pair from a Widowed Wife* (which Clay printed) had run into eight editions by 1850. On the other hand Richard Clay printed for them a work, which though small – some 300 octavo pages – was of great sociological importance. It was *The Philosophy of Artificial and Compulsory Drinking Usage* (1839) by John Dunlop, who was president of the General Temperance Union of Scotland. Instead of inveighing against alcohol Dunlop had set himself the task of investigating the drinking customs of ninety-eight trades and crafts in the British Isles and the result is a fascinating document. Dunlop's point was that the often compulsory convivial laws of the crafts started young people on the path of drunkenness at an early age. The influence of the book was such that groups of workmen began to refuse to take part in drinking festivities, urging that the money collected be used to build up 'mechanics' libraries'. As to printers Dunlop stated: 'There is considerable drinking on the pay-night among this class,' and in Ireland it was apparently the custom to subscribe for a drink even when a new fount of type was bought for the office. English chapel customs are detailed, money being deducted for the most diverse reasons – a youth having to pay a shilling into the fund the first time he was shaved.

Another publisher–customer, A. H. Baily, of Cornhill (for whom Clay printed *Wanderings in the Highlands and Islands* by W. H. Maxwell in 1844), provides a good example of the work for which Clay's stereotyping plant was particularly suited. This was the mass production of publishers' 'advertisements'. These announcements of a publisher's stock-in-trade and future publications could be printed in large quantities to be inserted in all books published. They were common in the nineteenth century but become less common after 1915. A good example is included in *Wanderings in the Highlands.* Printed by Clay, this 16-page 'advertisement' of Baily's other books indicates the neat typography of the time, particularly the use of black-letter and outline display faces.

In 1861 Clay printed for Richard Bentley ('Publisher in Ordinary to Her Majesty') a 600-page work *Carthage and Her Remains* by Dr N. Davis. This was an account of the excavations under the auspices of the British Government, and is one of the more substantial works of the period. Illustrated with some thirty bound-in engravings, it was bound by Edmonds and Remnants. This was because the period was one in which wholesale binders were most active. The book carries a printer's mark which does not seem to have been used for very long. It consists of a shield bearing the entwined initials 'R.C.' with an open book and flame as a crest. On ribbons are the name and address of the printer and a motto: 'Sola Lux Mihi Laus'. The mark was, however, used as the basis of the firm's seal when a limited company was formed.

Still in the possession of Clays is a copy of *Uncle Tom's Cabin,* by Harriet Beecher Stowe, printed by them for George Routledge in 1852. This must have been a very early English edition as it appeared in book form in America only in the March of that year.

Before the invention of process engraving Clays were renowned for their expert printing of wood engravings. As early as 1837 they had printed for their old customer, Thomas Kelly, an impressive two-volume *Engineers' and Mechanics' Encyclopaedia,* heavily illustrated with wood engravings. The date indicates that the engravings were probably printed from direct but this would not be the case after about 1840 as the electrotyping process had been developed the year before. William Savage in his *Dictionary of Printing* (1841) shows illustrations by the process. An impression of wax was taken of a wood engraving, covered with powdered plumbago, and suspended in a galvanic bath in which copper was present in a state of

A FOUR-OARED boat-race took place on Saturday the 16th instant, between the employés of Messrs. Clay, printers, Bread Street Hill, the course being from Westminster Bridge to Battersea Park Bridge, the prizes competed for being five silver cups.

The Fleet Street Gazette Vol. 1 No. 7 Saturday, May 23, 1874

WORKSHOP WHISPERINGS

THE result of the boat race between bookbinders from the Ship works and printers from Messrs. R. Clay & Sons, was disaster for the binders, the printers winning easily enough. On the day before the race nothing was known of any need for change in the composition of the Ship crew until the evening, when it was found that No. 3 would not be able to row, being seriously ill. Bow was then shifted into No. 3's place and a new man put into bow's place. When a start was effected, the Ship crew got away well, and after about a hundred yards drew away and led for a little, then they began to get mixed up, and very shortly the crew appeared completely paralyzed, losing eventually by about ten lengths. The steamer Victoria followed the race with a large company on board, including a good many representatives of the fair sex.

The British Bookmaker Vol. IV No. 38 August, 1890

The boat races

solution. The copper, affected by the electricity, left the solution and deposited itself on the face of the wax mould. The copper shell was then backed up with other metal to form a printing plate. Clays had an extensive electrotyping department, details of which are still known, but it is not known precisely when it was installed. The advent of mechanically driven printing machines, particularly the cylinder type, which would deal harshly with original wood engravings, and the need for bigger editions, would have indicated at an early date the desirability of making electrotypes and thus saving the original engravings.

During the years 1861 to 1863 Clays printed five volumes of the Rev. J. G. Wood's *Illustrated Natural History*. During the period of publication, the well-known Dalziel brothers, who were responsible for the engravings, went to see the author every Monday morning accompanied by the publisher, George Routledge, to report progress. They then went on to Clay's printing office, where the work was being printed under their supervision. This was significant because the Dalziels had set up their own press in Camden Town to make sure their engravings were printed to their satisfaction but Routledge obviously thought that Clays could do as well. In 1861 also Clays printed for Henry G. Bohn John Johnson's *A Treatise on Wood Engraving* which ran to 664 pages, 7 inches deep by 5 inches wide.

The miniature illustrated editions of Dickens printed for Chapman and Hall showed how well Clays could print rather fine wood engravings, although the small type of the editions is not attractive.

Clays began to achieve a particular reputation for the printing of colourful gift books, often elaborately illustrated and bound. In this respect they were fortunate in having the co-operation of Joseph Cundall (1818–95) a publisher, editor and book designer. He either published on his own behalf or firms such as Sampson Low published for him. He also designed books for various publishers. Mr Ruari McLean who has made a study of Cundall and of Victorian book design[1] has endeavoured to list books which were supervised or published by Cundall after 1852, the majority of which seem to have been printed by Clays. Particularly striking among these is *The Vicar of Wakefield*, illustrated by George Thomas, and published by

Sampson Low for Cundall in 1855. Other Clay/Cundall productions for Sampson Low include *The Pleasures of Hope* (1855), *The Rime of the Ancient Mariner* (1857), *The Farmer's Boy* (1857), *The Poetical Works of Edgar Allan Poe* (1858), *Favourite English Poems* (1859), *Poetical Works of T. Gray* (1859) and *The Merchant of Venice* (1860). For the publisher Bogue they produced in 1857 *Rhymes and Roundelays*, for Bell & Daldy *Poems and Songs* by Burns in 1858, for Routledge *Poems of William Wordsworth* in 1859 and for Ward Lock *Old English Ballads* in 1864.

Other lavishly decorated gift books were printed by Clays, often embellished by such artists as Henry Shaw. These included an edition of the *New Testament*, first published by Longmans in 1865, and *Two Centuries of Song* (Sampson Low, 1867). Mr McLean comments: 'Both volumes are unusual examples of mid-Victorian commercial design, and in both books the superb letterpress machining of Richard Clay made a vital contribution.'[2] He also mentions *Lalla Rookh* published by Longmans in 1861, and printed by Clays, which contained no less than 69 illustrations by Tenniel.

Other books of this type printed by Clays during this period included *Gertrude of Wyoming* (Routledge, 1857), and *The Poets of the West* (Sampson Low, 1859).

Cundall was appointed superintendent of the *Illustrated Catalogue* of the International Exhibition in London in 1862. The work was published in four volumes and the printing was shared out among five firms (Clay, Clowes, Edmund Evans, Petter and Galpin and Spottiswoode). Richard Clay was those among the guarantors of the exhibition for £300 (the Prince Consort guaranteed £10,000). A French commentator, M. Ch. Laboulaye, reporting on the exhibition referred to 'The Admirable wood-cut printing from Messrs. Clay's and Taylor's.'[3]

In 1885 Clays purchased for £400 the copyright of Cundall's series *Illustrated Biographies of Great Artists* which continued to be part of their stock-in-trade.

There is a general feeling in the trade that Victorian printing was very bad and had to be rescued by William Morris, yet Mr McLean obviously does not think so, and an examination of books printed by Richard Clay's firm during the middle part of the nineteenth century shows that, whatever one thinks of the style of design, the printing was of a high standard. It may be left to Dr John Johnson, Printer to the University of Oxford from 1925 to 1947, to have the last word. In his J. M. Dent Memorial Lecture in October 1933, he had this to say: 'Would any one deny perfection to the original issue of Palgrave's *Golden Treasury*, printed by R. Clay & Son in 1861 and published by Macmillan, which gathers into itself all the elegance of an age?'

Richard Clay junior did not receive a University education but joined his father's firm at 15 years of age in 1854, being apprenticed to his brother, Charles John. While Richard junior was to have a considerable effect on the technical development of the firm this did not become apparent at once. The senior Richard Clay was by now 65 years of age and although he was to live another 23 years the running of the business increasingly devolved on Joseph Taylor, who became a partner in 1857, the firm being known as Clay and Taylor, although the imprint was sometimes simply 'Richard Clay'.

In 1868 Richard Clay senior retired and the two sons formed a new partnership with Taylor, trading as R. Clay, Sons and Taylor. For a time Taylor was the dominant figure, Charles John being concerned with his partnership with Cambridge University (dealt with in the next chapter) and Richard junior gradually accumulating experience. Taylor replaced Richard Clay senior on the committee of the London Master Printers Association, but his touch was not sure in labour matters. He involved Clays in one of the few industrial disputes which the firm had with its employees. It was perhaps unfortunate for him that the association of master printers was breaking up because it could not agree on labour matters. It formally dissolved in October 1870. In 1866 the Compositors' Scale had been revised by agreement with the employers but early in 1870 one of the signatories, Gilbert and Rivington, repudiated the scale, giving as their reason their inability to compete with country houses. Taylor thought it a good idea to follow Gilbert and Rivington and revert to the scale of 1847. Union compositors refused to accept a cut in wages and were dismissed. But Clays found themselves alone with Gilbert & Rivington, there being no organised opposition to the 1866 scale.

Thereafter the compositors' union either dealt with individual firms, or the major firms would form a negotiating committee. In 1890 a new master printers' organisation was formed known as the Printing and Allied Trades Association, and this conducted negotiations with the unions. Peace was made between Clays and the London Society of Compositors in 1907. The men joined the union and the firm discontinued its donation to the National Free Labour Association.

What his partners thought of Taylor's actions is not known. He eventually retired and died before 1887, for in that year payment to his executors is included among the debts which the new limited company took over.

Richard Clay II (as he might be conveniently called) was among the most technically minded printers of his day and carried on the tradition that the firm be in the vanguard of technical development. He was responsible for a number of inventions. In 1872 he patented his improvements to the 'Wharfedale' type of cylinder machine. He explained: 'The object is to make a printing machine of the class mentioned with very slight adjustment to print sheets of any size from the smallest to the largest for which the machine is constructed. For this purpose I substitute for the "grippers" endless tapes which carry sheets to and fro under the cylinder and deliver them out after they have been printed. Further, in so modifying the arrangement of the tapes on one side of the cylinder as to convert the machine into a "perfecting machine". Hitherto reversal of sheets has been affected by hand. The machine is now capable of reversing the sheet for perfecting.' Perfecting is the term used by printers to indicate printing on both sides of the sheet. Richard Clay II also invented a system of holding down stereotype plates by atmospheric pressure.[4] A keen military volunteer (rising from the ranks of the Hornsey Corps to lieutenant-colonel) he was an expert shot. This explains his 1867 patent which related not to printing but to the breech loading of arms.

Further consideration will be given to the technical development back the second brush the roller travels down the inclined plane on to the third or " drying " cylinder and against the third brush.

[*Printed*, 6*d*. *Drawing*.]

A.D. 1872, September 13.—No. 2716

CLAY, Richard the younger.—" Improvements in printing " machines " known as " Wharfedale printing machines or " double feeding single cylinder machines."

In the first part of the invention an arrangement is claimed which enables such machines " to print sheets of any size " from the largest for which the machine is constructed to any " size smaller:"—Endless tapes are substituted for the grippers; these carry the sheets to and under the cylinder and deliver them out after they have been printed. Two sets of main tapes or tapes " by which the sheets are carried under " the cylinder " are used; the one set " passes around the " cylinder," the other " under the said cylinder and in contact " with the first named." Two other sets (each of three tapes " arranged one over another ") are employed, " one set at " each side of the cylinder." The first (or uppermost) of the three " pass over pulleys carried by arms or sectors, which " are capable of alternate oscillatory motion in a vertical " plane," and over a dropping bar, " by the action of which " the sheets are drawn in " between the first and second. The second pass over pulleys on the said sectors, " under and " in proximity to " the pulleys which carry the first, and thence " over a feeding drum." The third pass over pulleys " mounted on a shaft carried by the sectors under and in " proximity to the pulleys " which carry the second. The lower sides of the first and the upper sides of the second " constitute the feeding tapes," which carry the sheets to be printed to the main tapes. The lower sides of the second and the upper sides of the third " constitute the delivering tapes," which take the printed sheets from the main tapes and deliver them out of the machine. The sectors are alternately raised and lowered by cams so as to bring the first and second tapes at one side of the cylinder opposite the main tapes at that side, and the second and third tapes at the other side opposite

PRINTING 289

the main tapes at that side. " When the cylinder is reversed, " the reversion actions take place."

The claim made in the second part " consists in so modify- " ing the arrangement of the tapes at one side of the cylinder " as to convert the machine into a perfecting machine:"— Two sets of endless tapes are substituted for the set of three tapes at one side of the cylinder; one set " passes round the " feeding drum at that side and round the middle pulleys " carried by the sectors;" the other passes " round the said " drum (outside the first set)," and thence " round the upper " and under pulleys " mounted on the sectors. The blank sheet, fed between the first and second tapes, is carried by them into the main tapes, and by these under the cylinder. The main tapes carry the sheet printed on one side " to the " reversing tapes at the other side of the cylinder;" these carry the sheet " round the feeding drum " (thereby reversing the sheet) and " deliver it back to the main tapes, which on " the reversal of the machine carry the said sheet under the " cylinder, blank face downward." The main tapes carry the delivering tapes on that side of the cylinder from which the sheet was fed.

[*Printed*, 2*s*. *Drawings*.]

Patent specification of the Richard Clay II invention

of the firm but it is desirable at this point in the narrative to go back and trace the fortunes of Charles John, the founder's eldest son, and his descendants.

NOTES

1. See *Joseph Cundall: A Victorian editor, designer and publisher* by Ruari McLean. *Penrose Annual* Vol. 56, 1962; and *Victorian Book Design and Colour Printing* by the same author. Faber and Faber, 1963.

2. *Victorian Book Design and Colour Printing.*

3. *The Printers' Register*, October 1st 1864.

4. Richard Clay's apparatus was shown at the Caxton Celebration Exhibition, South Kensington, in 1877. The organisers appreciated historic continuity by including this and other systems along with stereotype plates of the Revd. Johann Muller, William Ged, Andrew Wilson (Stanhope's printer) and of Stanhope himself, as well as an 1805 example from the Cambridge University Press, but they probably did not realise the Clay connection with Stanhope or the Press or it would have been mentioned in the catalogue.

CHAPTER FIVE

The 'Cambridge' Clays

FOLLOWING THE RESIGNATION of Watts as Printer to the University of Cambridge in 1809 he was succeeded by John Smith, who held the office for 26 years. During his time the existing building had become inadequate to the growing business of the Press and a new printing-house was completed in 1827. Then it was proposed that surplus money subscribed some years before for the erection of a statue to the memory of William Pitt should be used to provide a new building entirely for the Press. The first stone of what was to be known as the Pitt Press building was laid in October 1831, and the work was completed in about eighteen months.

By 1827, however, the Syndics felt that Smith was not adequate to control the growing business, whatever his technical abilities. They resolved to consult various London printers and booksellers as to the expediency of appointing a superintendent of all departments of the Press. William Clowes, perhaps one of the most technically advanced printers of the time was asked to inspect the Press. He felt he had too many commitments in London and sent his manager, John Parker, in his place. Clowes was appointed superintendent and looked after the London end of the business while Parker was in charge in Cambridge. Parker brought new life to the Press and when John Smith eventually retired in 1836 he was appointed Printer in his place. Among Parker's innovations was to establish a depository for the sale of Cambridge Bibles in the Strand, in London; and under his control the publishing activities of the Press began to expand. Parker retired in 1854, having served the Syndics as both Printer and publisher.

This account has been provided as a background to developments with which the Clay family was concerned. One branch became firmly attached to the University Press and while it might be thought that they have no place in this history the fact is that members of this branch kept their interest in the family firm as partners, shareholders or directors and for many years a 'Cambridge' Clay acted as chairman of the London business. Moreover, there was a certain amount of interchange in operatives and in work. It is therefore desirable to trace the activities of Charles John (eldest son of the first Richard) and his descendants.

The University Commissioners of 1850–2 had reported that only by association in some form of co-partnership with printers or publishers could the University expect any considerable return on the capital invested in the Press. Accordingly, when Parker retired the Syndics began to look for such partners. Charles John Clay had just become engaged to Emily Jane, the daughter of a Hornsey neighbour, William Eady, a diamond merchant and, according to Clay's daughter, Mary Aimée, had begun to look out for a post sufficiently remunerative to allow him to marry. She also states that there were posts going at both Oxford and Cambridge 'and it was uncertain for a time which appointment he would obtain'. It looks as if Richard Clay's influence was at work because the Syndics recommended that the University enter into a partnership with Mr George Seeley, Fleet Street bookseller, and 'Mr Charles John Clay, M.A., of Trinity College and of Bread Street Hill, Printer'. This was agreed on July 3rd 1854.

Exactly why Charles John Clay received the appointment is not known, but it is possible that the Syndics were impressed by the fact that he was both a graduate of the University and a printer – as is shown by his description in the agreement. That this was so is underlined by a paragraph in a report the Syndics made to the Senate in October 1861, when C. J. Clay was asking to be allowed to live in London. It read: 'The Syndics are of the opinion that it is of great advantage to the Press and the University to have the management of the Press entrusted to a Graduate of the University and a Classical Scholar of Mr Clay's attainments.' The fact that his father and grandfather were men of Cambridge may have helped. The Syndics seemed later to be impressed by Richard Clay's standing as a printer. In the Senate report he is referred to as 'an eminent printer in London'. Equally important, no doubt, was the fact that he had the money to buy his son the partnership, for Charles John, about to marry and without a job, would be unlikely to raise the amount required himself. The agreement provided that Seeley should receive a commission of 12 per cent on Bibles and prayer books sold to the public and 2½ per cent on copies sold to societies; and that C. J. Clay should receive £400 a year as manager of the printing-house. The University put £10000 into the business and each partner, £5000, on which each contributor was to receive 5 per cent. Net profits were to be divided – half to the University and half equally between the two partners. In modern terms the sums of money were very large and to be able to put up £5000 for his son after paying for a University education would seem to indicate that Richard Clay's London business had become very prosperous in the quarter of a century since he left Devonshire Street.

Charles John had been born in the Devonshire Street premises but experienced the family's increasing prosperity as it moved to more pleasant surroundings. As soon as he obtained the Cambridge post he decided on marriage and the wedding took place at Hornsey on August 16th 1854.

Whatever was in the minds of the Syndics when they appointed him they had no reason to repent their decision. After only four years experience at Bread Street Hill he turned out to be an excellent Printer. His father went up to Cambridge with him and gave him valuable help and advice in the early days.

Seeley retired from the partnership in 1856 and the Syndics had sufficient confidence in Clay to give him a new agreement in which he was designated University Printer and Managing Partner of the Press. Various booksellers were appointed in succession to Seeley but the time had not yet arrived when the publishing side would demand a change in the partnership.

Charles John and Emily Jane Clay had five children – three girls and two boys. The oldest girl, Mary Aimée, was born in October 1855, and was responsible for collecting together information on the family. The two sons John (born January 1858) and Charles Felix (born November 1861) were to follow their father into the University partnership.

John Clay went to Marlborough and then on to St John's College, Cambridge, graduating M.A. He married Mary Hamblin Smith of Cambridge in 1882 and they had two sons, John Hamblin and Barnard Augustine, both of whom worked for the family firm. At the age of 24, in 1882, John Clay was admitted to the partnership with the University and from 1886 to 1904 the younger son, Charles Felix, was also associated with it.

Charles John was a success as Printer. In their report to the Senate of October 30th 1861 the Syndics stated: 'They consider it moreover due to Mr Clay to say that during the seven years of his management of the Press, he has conducted the business to their entire satisfaction; and that the financial condition of the Press, from having been most deplorable when he undertook the business, has become more prosperous than the most sanguine of those who promoted the present system of management could have hoped for.'

The period of his management was one of great expansion, output increasing five-fold in the first ten years. In 1863 a new foundry was built; in 1871 new machine rooms and warehouses were added and in 1877–8 a further three-storeyed building was erected. In 1886 large additions had to be made to the machinery and plant.

One of the most remarkable personalities connected with the Press in the nineteenth century was Alfred Mason, the manager, who, when he retired in 1919, had been at the Press for 65 years. From reminiscences of retired employees it is clear that both Charles John and, more particularly, John Clay leaned heavily on Mason for the actual administration of the Press, although maintaining a firm hand on general policy. We have evocative descriptions of Mason and the Clays and of nineteenth-century conditions in *A Stickful of Nonpareil*[1] written by George Scurfield from recollections of Arthur Dent and George Willers. The title of the book comes from one of Mason's favourite phrases, for a 'stickful of nonpareil' stood for a substantial helping of something or other – generally reproof. A stick is the receptacle in which a compositor sets type and nonpareil was the name of one of the smallest type sizes.

Both Clays were generally remote from the working staff, except on special occasions and appeared to have little idea of what would now be called 'personal relations'. Apprentices, in particular, were regarded as of little importance and there was the suspicion that they were idle by nature, as the following passages show: 'When the Old Man (Mr C. J. Clay) moved out to his house at Little Shelford, which he did in the summer months, one boy used to be employed every day in taking his *Times* and his letters out to him. This meant walking five miles each way. Sometimes, if the cook was in a good humour, the boy got a cup of cocoa with a bit of bread and cheese before he started back. When Mr Clay remembered, the boy was given threepence so that he could come back on the train; but this was an infrequent practice.

'When he made his daily tour of inspection Mr Clay carried an umbrella with which he prodded any boy he came across, telling him to "get a hustle on there".'

Like other members of his family Clay was very keen on the Volunteers and 'D' Company consisted of men from the Press. Mason, himself a Volunteer, would send for those who had not yet joined and point out that their prospects of being kept on at the Press would be greatly strengthened if Mr Clay knew they were Volunteers too.

There is an amusing passage about the Volunteers: 'On the occasion of the Shah of Persia rag Mr C. J. Clay received an urgent message from the Mayor asking him to turn out all he could of his company to form a guard of honour to welcome the Shah. Men were sent hurrying home to get into uniform and Mr Clay himself did the same, marching with his company and any members of the band it had been possible to collect, to the station. They were lined up in position and waited for the train to arrive, only to discover that the whole affair was an undergraduate hoax.'

John Clay followed his father's approach in labour relations as the the following shows: 'Mr John Clay, the second of his family to be University Printer, was a big man all round. He cannot have weighed much less than sixteen stone and with his great broad shoulders and his deep chest did not perhaps look his full height, which must have been about six foot. His face was ruddy and clean shaven except for the long, somewhat drooping moustaches.

'In common maybe with other employers of the time, he cultivated an air of aloofness and unapproachableness. On his daily tour of inspection, he was rarely if ever seen to speak to any member of the staff below the rank of clicker or storekeeper, unless he happened to catch a man misbehaving or playing the fool.

'He took no interest whatsoever in boys until they became apprentices and even then he would not speak to them. But, on his round, he would stand in front of a new apprentice and watch him at his work. With his feet apart and his hands clasped under the skirts of his jacket behind his back he would stare at the boy until he was sure that he knew him. And then he would grunt, and continue his round.

'This close inspection must have been very unnerving for the apprentice. More than one boy broke under the strain and burst into tears.

'He was always known as "Bull's Head" by the staff, and warning of his approach every morning was hoarsely stage-whispered from room to room. "Bull's Head!" meant that everyone was quiet and working industriously when he entered a room. He was very regular in his visits and must have known the staff were ready for him.

'It was quite unheard of to approach Mr Clay in person; no one ever went to his office unless sent for. Most of the staff lived and worked in a state of apprehension, always frightened that they might have incurred his displeasure, always afraid of being dismissed. But in fact no one was turned off during his reign at the Press except for serious misbehaviour, so that, considering the times, it would seem that he was a good and just employer. The harshness of his discipline could surely have been paralleled in almost every other works and business in the country.

'He was very proud of his position and of the business, and he was always jovial and amiable on social occasions. With his 'Widdicombe Fair' he certainly made his contribution to the fun of the wayzgoose dinners.'

The discipline does seem harsh today. On one occasion, according to George Willers,[2] a very old reader who had made two mistakes in a Bible proof was reduced to the composing room and a very low rate of pay at a minute's notice. There were no paid holidays until after 1916 when the Partnership ended. On the other hand, employment at the Press was greatly prized and the pay was higher than many other similar occupations.

In October 1861 C. J. Clay approached the Syndics and asked them for a relaxation of his agreement with them. This agreement, of 1856, obliged him to live in Cambridge and restrained him from being a partner in any other business. Clay wanted to become a partner in his father's business at Bread Street Hill. Richard Clay was by now in his seventies, Taylor was getting on in years and Charles John wanted to assist his brother. There was also the possibility that the father might die or retire – in which case Charles John would succeed to a large part of the business. As part of this change he also wanted to be allowed to live in London.

The Syndics originally agreed. They felt that the business of the Press did not require Clay's constant presence in Cambridge as it did at first, and the publishing business in London could be carried out by him rather than by an agent. The Syndics consulted a solicitor to see whether Clay's partnership with his father would involve the University in any pecuniary responsibility not connected with the Press. The solicitor reported: 'I regard it as very clear that no pecuniary responsibility on account of the London House can in any contingency result to the University by reason of his (Mr Clay's) concurrent Partnership with them in the Pitt Press business.' The Syndics pointed out that Clay had a large pecuniary stake in the Press and it would not answer his purpose to allow it to be unproductive and that he would continue to have a strong inducement to make the Press prosperous.

But by the next month the Syndics had changed their minds. Doubt had been expressed as to the expediency of permitting Clay to be resident in London and becoming a partner in his father's business. A compromise was reached by which Clay withdrew his application to change his residence and asked only that he could become a partner at Bread Street Hill. If this were agreed his

Telephone No. 1528.

Richard Clay & Sons, Limited,
London & Bungay.

Bread Street Hill,
Queen Victoria Street, E.C.

June 20/95.

Dear Sir,

I regret that you should have cause to complain about the reading of the Economic Journal proofs, but in the case of the figure on p. 196 it appears that it went out correctly in slip form, although we have not the slips now to refer to as proof, and was apparently corrected to 446 before being made up into pages, this figure in turn being corrected by Mr Higgs to 468 as it appeared in print. You should have received your copy of the Journal on Tuesday, but

I am afraid it would have been impossible to have sent it any earlier than that as we only received the last 3 sheets for press on Wednesday, on which there was a considerable amount of work to be done before they could be sent to the machine. In addition to this, Saturday being only ½ a day we were prevented from getting them ready for the Commissionaires by Monday morning and so could not start despatching them till Tuesday.

I am, Dear Sir,

Yours faithfully,

Cecil Clay

Professor Edgeworth.

Letter written to a customer in 1895

periodical visits to London could also be used to conduct the Bible business there.

In the event Clay did not at that point take up the agency in London which was held by booksellers for another ten years; but he did join his father, thus allowing the old man to retire in 1868. The founder of the business died at Muswell Hill in December 1877, in his 89th year. A new partnership was formed by Charles John and his brother Richard with Joseph Taylor, and following Taylor's retirement a limited company was formed in 1888 under the title of Richard Clay & Sons Ltd. The assets of the old partnership were transferred to the new company by the three brothers Charles John, Richard and Arthur Lloyd and the relative holdings of the two printer brothers is shown by the distribution of shares. Of the 976 ordinary shares they held 910 (Charles John – 480; Richard – 430). They held all the 3000 Preference shares (Charles John – 1718; Richard 1282) and all the 1000 Deferred shares (Charles John – 571; Richard – 429). The other shareholders were their younger brother, Arthur Lloyd (the Indian Civil Servant); Charles John's two sons, John and Charles Felix; Richard II's two sons – another Richard and Arthur Cecil (always known as 'Cecil'); and two relatives Thomas Eady and John Miles (Richard and Arthur Lloyd had married sisters, daughters of Joseph Miles of Highgate).

Returning to Cambridge affairs, the Syndics 'acting on the advice of Mr Clay', decided in 1872 that the time had come to set up their own publishing business, covering learned works and text books as well as prayer-books and Bibles, instead of using existing pubishers or booksellers as their agents. Premises were rented in Paternoster Row, but business increased to such an extent that a move to bigger premises in Ave Maria Lane became necessary in 1883.

Before this, because of the extension of the work of the Syndics, C. J. Clay offered to act as unpaid secretary to the Syndics. They agreed but were careful to add that the appointment did not convey any right to be present at the meetings of the Syndicate. The increasing business led to the admission to the partnership of the first son, John Clay, in 1882, and in 1886 of the second son, Charles Felix, with a view to his taking a share in the publishing side.

At the outset of C. J. Clay's career as Printer the Syndics had little to do except to authorise additions to the capital of the printing business. But it was Clay's very efficiency which enabled the Syndicate to extend its publishing activities, and in 1891, when they recognised that these had become too large to be effectively managed by their printing partner acting as a part-time secretary, they appointed a paid secretary. Clay is known to have been very annoyed by this move, in which he is reported to have 'acquiesced'.[3] This may have precipitated his decision to retire from the post of Printer at the end of 1894. In January 1895 at a characteristically brief ceremony at the Press the staff presented him with a silver salver, a silver inkstand and an address. Some speeches were made stressing the great contribution Clay had made to the Press; he replied briefly, shook the hands of a few old employees and left.

He had a final moment of glory in 1897 when he was elected Master of the Stationers Company in London. He died in 1905.

On Charles John's retirement the University entered into a partnership with his sons, John (to act as University Printer) and Charles Felix (as manager of the London publishing house). In January 1903 the Syndics appointed a sub-syndicate to consider whether to carry on the partnership with the Clay brothers or any other persons after the expiration of the agreement. They wanted to see whether the Press was losing work because of high prices. They therefore asked R. MacLehose a well-known printer of Glasgow, to report on the management of the Press. What the Syndics expected MacLehose to find is not known because he finally reported that considering the difficulties arising particularly from the awkward layout of the buildings the printing charges of the Press were not unreasonable; and that he thought the machine room and foundry were excellent. The profits for 1902 were up on those of 1901 and 1900 as a result of the installation of new machinery. The sub-syndicate reported: 'The sub-syndicate are of the opinion that Mr Clay has shown both judgement and enterprise in recommending the purchase of these machines,' and they recommended the continuation of John Clay's management of the printing side. But they also reported that C. F. Clay's share in the management of the Press

Richard Clay II

J. Miles

C. J. Clay

John Clay II

A. Cecil Clay

Richard Clay III

Arthur L. Clay

Charles Felix Clay

Archibald G. Clay

J. Hamblin Clay

Richard Clay IV

A. D. Newbery

H. E. Bowerbank

F. W. R. Douglas

P. N. Davis

Miss J. Robbins

was very small, due to time taken up with publishing. Therefore in 1904 changes were proposed. John Clay's partnership was renewed, but the publishing partnership was dissolved and the London business consolidated with C. F. Clay as manager.

John Clay like others of his family had a good eye for machinery and technical advances. He was not so adept when it came to the aesthetic side of printing. His one essay in type design – the so-called Cambridge type – was based on earlier forms and can hardly be said to have been a success. It can be seen in his *A Short Note on the Cambridge University Press* (1911), in which it is stated: 'The type used in this pamphlet was prepared by photographing every letter of the alphabet from a 15th-century printed book in the University Library. These photographs were entrusted to a type-designer with instructions to cut a fount of type, following the photographs exactly, and only modernising the letters so as to make them uniform in thickness. It will be seen on comparing this type with that of the Kelmscott Press that there is considerable similarity between the two faces.' The only similarity is that of caricature, and D. B. Updike[4] sums it up best: 'As for the Cambridge type of the University Press, Cambridge, it is an unattractive letter, which combines many of the defects of the fonts we owe to the modern revival. It is difficult to see why it was ever cut at all.' The composition of the pamphlet, with exaggerated spacing between words does not say much for the typographical standards of the Press at the time.

After this experiment no further efforts in typography were made until in 1910, when there was a move to install composing machines. After discussion with the University Printer the Syndics agreed not to introduce these machines. However, in 1913 opinion changed and three 'Monotype' composing machines were acquired. In February 1916 a committee was appointed by the Syndics to consider typographical improvements, but before the whole matter could be fully aired the Syndics were faced with the sudden death of John Clay on March 20th. The Syndics then decided to dissolve the partnership and appoint a staff University Printer.

John Clay's shares in the family firm were left to his wife and to his son, John Hamblin Clay, who joined the board of directors and eventually became chairman.

Charles Felix Clay continued to be Manager of the London office of the University Press, which had moved in 1904 to even bigger premises in Fetter Lane (by 1921 the staff had risen in number to 110). He retired in 1925, but not before being President of the Publishers Association 1923–5. Like his father he became Master of the Stationers Company (in 1938). He also served as Alderman in Cambridge in 1926. His outside interests were surprisingly diverse – bee-keeping and fencing. He was Hon. Secretary of the Amateur Fencing Association 1900–5 and of the Epée Club 1901–5; and translated a book from the French *Secrets of the Sword* in 1900. He was for a long time a director of the family firm, serving as chairman. He died in February 1947, aged 85.

The Cambridge Clays were those who sought diligently to discover the family origins, a preoccupation they inherited from Richard, the first printer. He had for a long time a sketch of an alleged 'Clay' coat-of-arms the history of which was unsure. In 1864 he approached the College of Arms for an investigation. Thomas William King, York Herald at the time, found that the arms had no authority, but he offered to trace the origin of the family. This offer was not taken up, but C. J. Clay painstakingly made enquiries at his father's request. The arms which Richard possessed were supposed to be of Clay of Huntingdon and were: 'Argent a bend azure cottized or charged with two ducks proper between four mascles or. Crest a pheon's head.' York Herald said that the 'false heraldry as regards the colours and bearings' confirmed his opinion that the arms could never have been issued by authority. However, by 1898 the College of Arms registered a pedigree of the Clay family, but the King of Arms refused to take the origins further back than Thomas Clay of Cambridge, grandfather of Richard. Arms were, however, granted to Charles John Clay and it is amusing to see that they resemble the 'false heraldry' of Richard's version: 'Argent a bend dovetail between a book in chief and two mascles in base all azure. Crest upon a rock proper, a pheon azure, in front thereof a key fesseways ward upwards and to the sinister of the last.'

In other words the two ducks disappeared from the bend which was now dovetailed and two of the mascles were replaced by a book. The crest[5] was suitably altered but the main element – a pheon or arrow head – remained.

NOTES

1. *A Stickful of Nonpareil* written by George Scurfield; illustrated by Edward Ardizzone. Privately printed at the University Press, Cambridge, 1956. Passages from this work have been quoted with the kind permission of the University Printer.

2. Personal recollection.

3. *The Evolution of Cambridge Publishing* by S. C. Roberts. Cambridge University Press, 1956.

4. *Printing Types: Their History, Forms and Use.* Cambridge, Mass.: The Harvard University Press, 1922.

5. The Clay Crest:

The Linotype bay at the Chaucer Press (*circa* 1910)

CHAPTER SIX

Printing Equipment in the 'Eighties

CHARLES CHILDS DIED suddenly in 1876 and, there being no male heirs, his printing business in Bungay was purchased by Clays. The two firms had worked together for many years and this take-over was a natural development. It was a shrewd move on the part of Clays for several reasons. London book printers were increasingly having to face competition from Scotland and the provinces, and this was a constant theme in the negotiations covering the 1847 and 1866 Compositors' scale. The compositors reporting on their conference with the master printers in 1847 gave examples. One printer had lost fourteen or fifteen volumes to Oxford because he could not do the work at the price required, and another said he had estimated for some volumes which had gone to Bungay in Suffolk 'though his compositors were walking about for want of employment'. The master printers at their meeting on March 12th 1866 specifically stated that a general rise of London wages would increase the tendency of London publishers to employ provincial printing offices.

Whether the arguments put forward by the London master printers against wage increases in general were valid or not, provincial competition was a fact which had to be faced, particularly if certain London printers were moving into the provinces themselves. One of Clays' main rivals, the firm of Clowes, was aware of the problem and two young members of the family, W. C. K. Clowes and W. A. Clowes, had already decided to look around to see whether they could find a provincial firm for sale. In 1873 they went into partnership with William Moore, the proprietor of the Caxton Press at Beccles in Suffolk. It was a small works, with only four

The jobbing department composing room at Bread Street Hill

power-driven printing machines. After many troubles Clowes and Clowes as it was called, got on its feet and in 1880 amalgamated with the London firm, a limited company being formed under the name of William Clowes and Sons Ltd.[1]

But the Childs business was not small and had from its earliest days concentrated on new techniques, inspiring Richard Clay to do likewise. Machine printing was introduced in 1855 with four platens, made by Ross of Edinburgh, and then later with single and double cylinder machines. Childs of Bungay must also have been the earliest firm in Britain to install a composing machine. This point will be examined later. The Childs family had also been innovators in the publishing field, as early as 1826 issuing the 'Imperial Edition of Standard Authors' in parts, thus becoming pioneers of serial publication.

Clays therefore gained what was for the day an advanced works in the country, with its attendant economic advantages, a staff experienced in book production, a number of contracts and a large supply of stereotype plates.

By a piece of good fortune we are able to ascertain with a fair degree of accuracy the range of equipment held both in London and Bungay in the year 1887. Because the firm intended to become a limited company it was necessary for Charles John Clay and Richard Clay II to draw up a schedule of the partnership's assets for transfer to the new company, and this schedule has survived. Apart from its particular connection with the Clay history it also has a wider interest as it provides a record of two moderately sized printing establishments at a point in history when older techniques associated with the beginnings of printing were being used at the same time as those which continue to this day.

The very names of parts of the establishments indicate that traditional methods were still in use. That some paper was still being damped before printing is indicated by the existence of the 'wetting cellar' at Bread Street Hill. It contained a wetting trough with tables and a Harrild wetting machine, as well as iron plates and boards. At Bungay there was only an 'Old Wetting room', with 'old bench, pails etc.' which may mean that damping had been given up.

Both Clays and Childs were ahead of their time in the use of composing machines, and Childs may well have been the first regular user in Britain. The typesetting machine invented by Dr William Church (1822) is not known to have gone beyond the prototype stage and while the Young and Delcambre (1840) was certainly used to set a number of publications it was not, as far as is known, used in a regular printing office. The earliest American typesetting machine was that of W. H. Mitchel, of Brooklyn, who patented his machine in 1853. John F. Trow, a New York printer, installed twelve Mitchel machines in his office in 1855 and claimed his was the first printing office in the world where type was regularly set by machinery.

The following item under 'Bungay Plant' in the Clay schedule is therefore of special interest: 'A composing mach. by Mitchell [*sic*] wood frame complete.' Mitchel's machine had a wooden frame and looked rather like a grand piano. It is in the earliest group of composing machines and if the Bungay specimen had survived it would have been of major historical interest. It has not been generally appreciated that Mitchel machines were exported to Britain and since more advanced machines made of iron soon came on to the market, Childs must have had their Mitchel in the 1850s. They installed at least four iron-based machines, as is shown by other entries in the schedule, but unfortunately the make is not given. The entry concerning 'special nicked type' for a composing machine probably refers to the Mitchel machine.

In London Clays were always on the look-out for improvements in typesetting and were one of the few firms to install a Mackie steam type-composer, the first machine to use perforated tape commercially,[2] thus anticipating the 'Monotype' by about thirty years. It was in 1867 that Dr Alexander Mackie, of Warrington, applied the Jacquard system to typesetting. The perforator was like a small piano on which keys were struck to punch holes in a code in a spool of paper. This spool was fed into a steam-driven machine which carried boxes of type around a circular iron table. When the machine was set in motion the action of the perforated tape would cause the delivery of type to a point of delivery. Mackie and his friends used

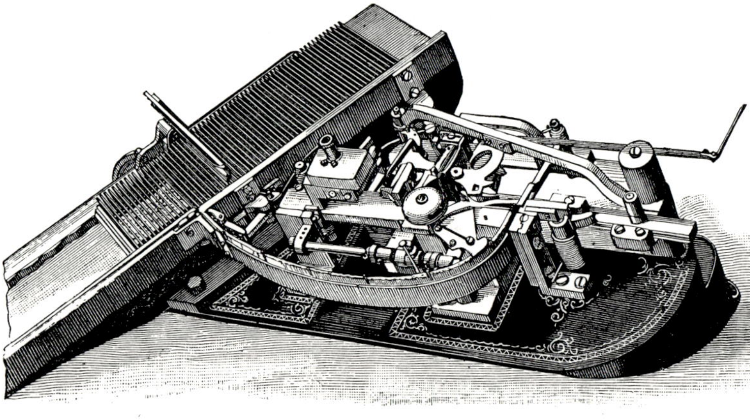

Lagerman 'Typotheter'

Lagerman justifying machine

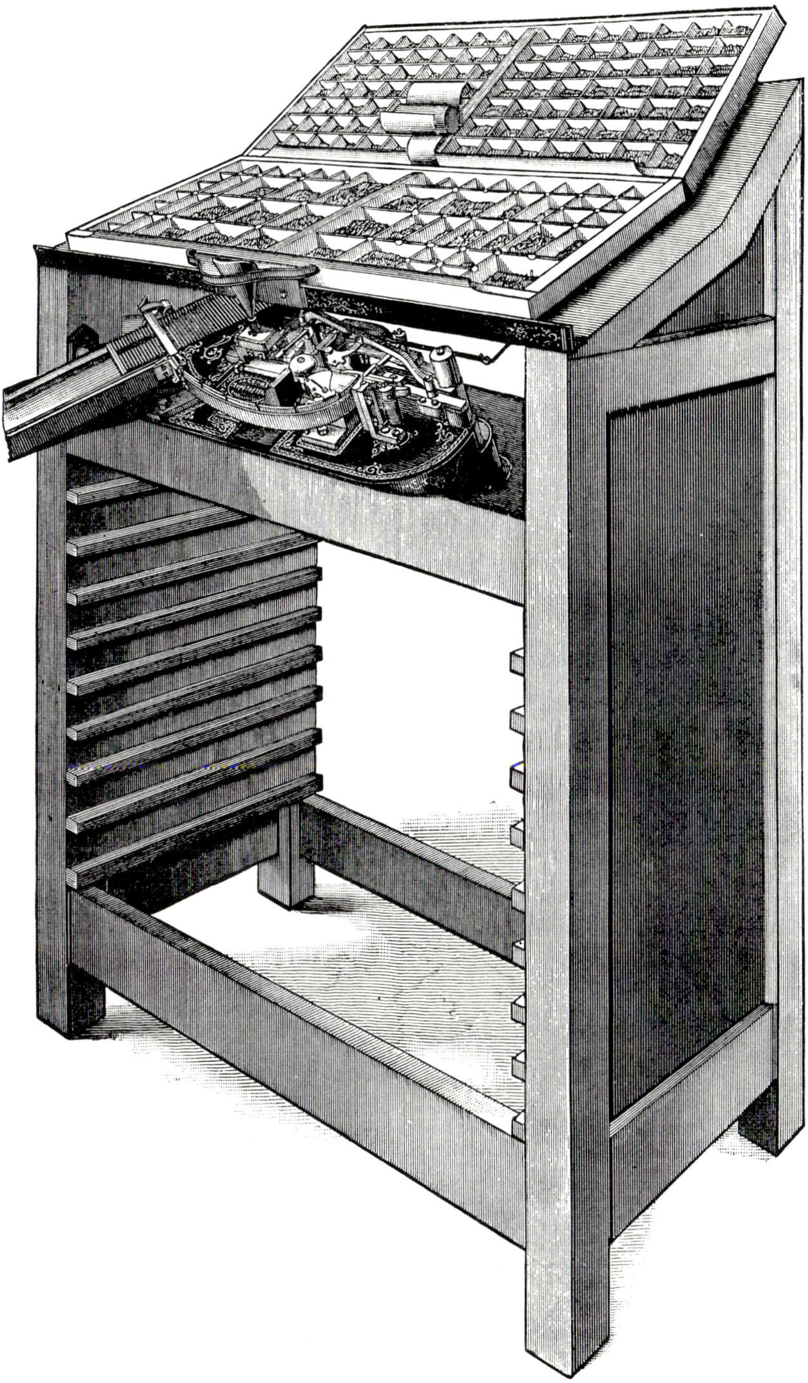

The Lagerman Typotheter in position on frame

the machine for their own newspapers and publications but Clays is the only firm known to have taken it up outside of Mackie and his circle. It was used to set the periodical, *The Graphic*, which Clays printed for a time, and was exhibited at the International Exhibition at the Albert Hall in 1871, being described in *The Graphic* of July 17th and of October 21st. By 1887 the machine had ceased to be manufactured and it looks as if Clays had written off their models. In the Schedule there is the entry: '2 Composing Machines Mackie . . . £50; Do . . . £20.' Mackie had charged at least £250 each for his machines.

Clays also tried out Lagerman's Typotheter the year after the Schedule was produced. Invented by Alexander Lagerman of Jönköping in Sweden, the Typotheter was a device to free the compositor's second hand when composing type – thus theoretically allowing him to work twice as fast using both hands. It was a mechanism which could be placed on a board beneath the ordinary type case. The compositor picked out pieces of type with both hands and dropped them into a funnel at the top of the Typotheter. A small motor caused a series of feelers to turn the type, face up, nick outwards, no matter how it was dropped, and forwarded it through a raceway to the galley. A bell rang when the line was full and this had to be transferred to another position to be justified.

On Friday, June 8th 1888, the King of Sweden called at Bread Street Hill to inspect the machine invented by his subject. After the visit, the secretary of the Lagerman Typotheter and Justifier Co. Ltd., Gustaf Hagborg, wrote to John Southward, a printing trade journal editor, on June 11th as follows: 'As to the visit of the King of Sweden and Norway to Messrs, Richard Clay & Sons I may mention that Dr John Evans, who is interested in the business, invited His Majesty to come to the City and I want especially to mention that the King took hold of Mr Clay's hand and pressing it firmly thanked him for the interest he had taken in this most wonderful Swedish invention. I feel confident that the invention will interest you very much and that the type-composing problem has now been practically solved.'[3] Mr Hagborg was to be disappointed. The apparatus failed as a commercial proposition because of the very small saving in time over the traditional hand method, and Clays had abandoned the Typotheter by 1895 as they informed Southward in a letter.

In various departments at Bread Street Hill there were a number of hand presses used either for proofing or for short-run work. In the Plate cellars there is listed simply '1 Hand Press Crown £5', but elsewhere the name of the maker is given. For example, in the Machine Room there were '2 Dble Crown Hand presses Hopkinson & Cope' (£40) together with '8 Extra Tympans and 19 Extra Friskets' (£10). The words 'machine' and 'press' were used more precisely than they are today and the Machine Rooms would normally contain machines for mass production and the Press Room hand presses for limited edition work. In Clays' Press Room there were a variety of hand presses including seven of the earliest all-metal press, the Stanhope (5 Super Royal at £25 each; 2 demy at £15 each). There were four double crown size (2 Napiers and 2 Columbians) at £40 each; four Super Royal Columbians at £25 each; 7 Super Royal Albions at £25 each and 2 Foolscap Albions at £25 each. A single Cropper platen press, listed at £45, was a forerunner of the platen presses which gradually replaced the hand press for small jobbing work. A lithographic printing press (£5) was for printing from stones,[4] 25 of which for a work on freemasonry were listed at five shillings each.

In the Machine Room there were 28 machines all designated by size and name but working on different principles. Still being used was the popular double platen machine which, while mechanically driven, still relied on the old principle of flat pressure. These machines were used for high quality work in preference to cylinder machines. Clays used a number of makes – Napier, Rich and Hopkinson – and they were mostly costed at as high a rate as the cylinder machines – Dryden, Hopkinson, Wharfedale, Newsum and Anglo-American. The firm still made some of its own inking rollers for these machines as there was a separate Roller Making Room containing 27 roller moulds.

The electrotype and stereotype foundry was well equipped. There was a separate 'Woodcut Room' but special 'fittings' were

Part of the stereotyping foundry at Bread Street Hill

kept in the foundry for making electros from original woodcuts and engravings.

At what stage Clays went over to the more modern method of stereotyping is not known exactly. Plaster moulds, as used by Lord Stanhope and his successors, had been superseded by papier mâché as early as 1846 in England. The sheet of paper mâché was placed on a type forme and beaten or rolled to obtain an impression from which the stereotype plate was cast. The first trade foundry to use the papier mâché method started up in 1855. We know that Clays were using papier mâché by at least 1870 because of Joseph Taylor's ill-fated attempt to repudiate the 1866 compositors' scale. There still exists, attached to his copy of the 1847 scale, a notice in his own hand, as follows: 'On and after Monday April 18, 1870 the Compositors in this Establishment will be paid according to the Scale of 1847 with the following exceptions 1. All Stereo plates and Standing matter to be the property of the House 2. No extra charge to be made for matter set up for Stereotyping.'

The reason for the exceptions was the changes in stereotyping technique since the signing of the 1847 agreement, which laid down: 'All matter Stereotyped by the present method, namely by using plaster of Paris, to be cast up, if with high spaces, at 1/4*d.* per 1000 additional; if with low spaces, at ½*d.* per thousand additional. Should any other method be adopted obviating the inconvenience experienced by the compositor, no extra charge per 1000 to be made; but if imposed in small chases, 1*s.* per sheet to be allowed.' Against 'should any other' Taylor has written in the margin 'papier mâché'.

The composing-room equipment indicates the vast quantities of foundry type required by a firm of this size before the general introduction of such machines as the 'Linotype' and 'Monotype'. Type was purchased from all the main typefounders and was also cast on the premises. Bungay was also supplied with type from this source. While there were three letter-casting machines, estimated at £200 each, hand moulds were still being used. Eleven letter moulds at £15 each and six space moulds at £15 or £12 (according to size) are listed, as well as matrices for various founts to the value of £253.

Type both in case and standing formes; chases and composing furniture were valued at the very large sum of £17,737.

The recorder at Bungay often provided more detail than his colleague at Bread Street Hill. Not only do we learn the names of various departmental heads ('Mr Cox's Room', 'Plate Correcting Room Mr Richards') but also the exact age of the hand presses. These included four Columbians made by the original inventor, George Clymer – two Double Crown, Nos. 265 and 283 of 1825 and two Royal (No. 223 of 1825 and No. 365 of 1828). There was also a Bevan model, a foolscap folio, dated 1861. Two Albion presses, dated 1837 and 1853, an Atlas (undated but by Wood and Sharwood, No. 34) completed the hand presses. In the 'Room over Foundry', where old equipment such as the composing machines was apparently kept there was an '18″ litho press top lever by Steelfox'. George A. Ferguson, writing in 1906, states that a lithographic press was used in the early days at Bungay, but was mainly used to reproduce copies of music for Charles Childs' 'Musical Society'. He also states that he saw several old Columbian presses, of which the only relics existing today are two 'eagle' counterweights on the top of entrance posts to a house outside Bungay.

Double platen machines also featured in the Bungay Machine Room. Still there were those made by Ross of Leith, which Charles Childs had introduced in 1855 as well as a similar machine by 'Rich'. Two Main machines and two Anglo-French perfectors completed the machine equipment.

The schedule is also a source of other information with regard to the copyrights held by Clays and as to what jobs were in hand at the time of its compilation. Reference will be made to it in later chapters. It is also the source of our knowledge that Bread Street Hill was already becoming overcrowded and that there was an overspill into rented premises. Clays held a lease of 14½ years from February 1883 on the basement of the Memorial Hall, Farringdon Street. It looks as if it were used for storage as no details of equipment used there is given, simply 'fittings', valued at £500. This basement was later used as a machine room by the St Bride Institute Printing School.

Clays were noted for their machine printing and just as men who had been trained at Bungay in stereotyping were proud to announce this, even in the United States, so to have been apprenticed as a machine manager at Clays was a valuable asset. When Stephen Austin, of Hertford, ordered a Main machine in 1861 he called on Richard Clay to find a machine man and was able to engage E. Gaskell. The head of the Oxford University Press machine department, George Hall, who died in 1899, was trained at Clays, and was specially expert with the double platen machines, which, it is noted in an obituary, were being superseded in favour of Wharfedale single-cylinders in the late eighties.

NOTES

1. Because of the similarity of name, location and work of the two big book-printing firms there has sometimes been confusion. A former member of the staff of Macmillan's, the publishers, told the story of two of their employees. One is said to have asked whether a book had been printed by 'Cloweses' and the other replied 'No, by Clayses, not Cloweses'.

2. See *An Assessment of Mackie's Steam Type-Composing Machine* by James Moran. Journal of the Printing Historical Society. No. 1. 1965.

3. John Southward's scrapbook on composing machines in the St Bride Printing Library, London.

4. Lithography: originally printing from a greasy image on stone, invented by Aloysius Senefelder in Munich in 1796. In commercial lithography today metal plates have been substituted for the stone and the printing is usually carried out on rotary presses.

CHAPTER SEVEN

The House of Macmillan

TWO YOUNG SCOTTISH booksellers, Daniel and Alexander Macmillan, published their first books from a London address in 1843, but their bookselling business was based on Cambridge. There followed a period when operations were divided between Cambridge and London until in 1863, after his brother's death, Alexander set up as a publisher in London.

Because of the Cambridge background the connection with the Clays was an early one. While in Cambridge the Macmillans had arranged for the printing of books by C. J. Clay at the University Press. In fact, the practice of scholars publishing with Macmillan and printing at the University Press became widely prevalent because of the slowness of the Syndics of the Press in awakening to their own potentialities as publishers.

The Macmillans met the London Clays through C. J. Clay and were soon distributing orders between the two printing houses. C. J. Clay printed *Pilgrim's Progress* in 1862 and Richard Clay was responsible for Palgrave's famous *Golden Treasury* the year before. Only 2000 copies were printed of the first edition, but the 1865 edition carries on the half title 'twenty-fifth thousand'. London was also used to print Roundall Palmer's *The Book of Praise* in 1862.

Earlier, Clays had been called upon to print *Macmillan's Magazine*, which commenced in 1859 and lasted until 1907. It was the first of the shilling monthlies, appearing two months before *Cornhill*. It combined political and religious articles with travel sketches, fiction and poetry. At first it held its own against *Blackwood's* and *Cornhill*. At one time it was edited by John Morley (later Viscount Morley), but when he had ceased to be editor, the policy changed, the focus shifting to literature and it tended to decline.

The printing of this magazine constituted a key point in Clays' development. While they had been responsible for the printing of small periodicals in the past (*The Herald of Peace* as early as 1824), *Macmillan's Magazine* set them on the path of popular periodical printing. By today's standards *Macmillan's Magazine* was not very striking. The setting was in two columns on a page 8 inches deep by 5¼ inches and, apart from an engraved title page, there were no illustrations. It was the quality of the contributors which attracted. Matthew Arnold wrote regularly from 1863 to 1887, Tennyson contributed poems and other writers included T. H. Huxley, R. L. Stevenson, W. M. Rossetti, Octavia Hill and Charles Kingsley.

Ten years after the launching of *Macmillan's Magazine* Macmillan's began the publication of the important weekly scientific journal, *Nature*, and Clays were asked to print it. The first issue came out on November 4th 1869 and for a period of more than fifty years, until December 1920, Clays were responsible for the production. Later Macmillans entrusted them with the *Journal of Hellenic Studies.*

Clays now had a reputation not only for book printing, but for periodical production and it is not surprising that just as *Nature* appeared they should be approached to print a new illustrated weekly, *The Graphic.* Periodical printing will be dealt with separately as it had much to do with the firm's later policy decisions. In the meantime it would be convenient to follow Macmillans in another periodical venture.

The success of illustrated magazines caused them to think that this was a field which they should enter. They therefore proposed to Clays that they should join with them in bringing out a monthly entitled the *English Illustrated Magazine.* A memorandum of agreement was drawn up on January 27th 1883 and Clays invested the odd capital sum of £6,889. 14*s.* There were regular losses on the magazine, and by 1887, when the schedule was drawn up, Clays reckoned their investment was worth only £4,355. 7*s.* 9*d.* In 1891 they calculated their share of the loss that year as £827. 3*s.* 9*d.*

Technically the magazine represented the transition from wood engraving to the half-tone process. While not striking typographically (it was set in the usual two columns) it contained a remarkable range of engravings from originals by well-known artists – Walter Crane, Harry Furniss, Randolph Caldecott, Charles Whymper, George du Maurier and Joseph Pennell. The printing was of a high quality and the engravers had reached the height of their technique, even reproducing pencil and chalk drawings with fidelity. The illustrations were superintended by Emery Walker, adviser to William Morris at the Kelmscott Press and a pioneer process engraver. But the editorial content could not have been over-popular. As Charles Morgan says in the history of Macmillans,[1] it tended to be nostalgic – with stately houses and old coaching days as its subjects – and it never clearly made up its mind what its purpose was. There were divisions of policy and compromises were made – of the type which are always considered when a publication is in difficulty. Articles were carried on the affairs of major advertisers, which provoked criticism from readers. Macmillans kept the magazine going for nearly ten years but in 1892 it was sold to Edward Arnold of Bedford Street, the Strand. Clays continued to print the magazine for the new proprietor. A year was enough for him, however, and he sold the *English Illustrated Magazine* to his near-neighbours, Ingram Brothers, the proprietors of the very successful *Illustrated London News*, who no doubt considered themselves specialists in that kind of publication. They allowed Clays to keep the printing contract for another year, but in 1895 they decided to take over the printing themselves. This pattern was to repeat itself later in relation to the *Illustrated London News*. In 1897, as an experiment, the *English Illustrated Magazine* was handed over to the 20-year-old Bruce Ingram, son of the managing director, Sir William Ingram. It lost the young man money and so he handed it over to the publisher, Fisher Unwin, who kept it going until 1913. By the time Clays ceased printing the *English Illustrated Magazine* a strange mixture of engraving processes was being used – even original photographs being reproduced by wood engraving when the half-tone process, also used, would have been more suitable. Clays' contact with Bruce Ingram, who began editing the *Illustrated London News* for his father and uncle in 1900, was to bear fruit in 1905 when they obtained the contract for printing the weekly.

To return to Macmillans – it was as a consequence of its connection with this firm that Clays became involved in the controversial printing of Lewis Carroll's *Alice's Adventures in Wonderland*, one of those subjects dear to the heart of bibliographers and bibliophiles, not forgetting antiquarian booksellers. For Clays it was to prove a profitable undertaking in the future.

As told by Charles Morgan,[2] 'Carroll', the Revd. Charles Lutwidge Dodgson, a mathematics don at Christ Church, made an arrangement with the University Press at Oxford to produce *Alice*. Fifty of the 2000 copies were to be delivered in advance for Dodgson's young friends. When 48 copies had been given away the author declared himself dissatisfied with the printing of the text and Tenniel illustrations, recalled the copies, cancelled the edition and 'shipped off the 1952 unbound sheets to Messrs. Appleton of New York.' Some of the presentation copies were not returned and have since made fantastic prices at auctions. When the sheets had been sent to America, Richard Clay prepared another edition, dated 1866 and *Alice* began its best-selling career.

However, a more careful and detailed account is given by W. H. Bond in the *Harvard Library Bulletin*, Autumn 1956. Macmillans entered the picture as it had been agreed that they would publish the book on commission. According to Bond, Dodgson saw nothing wrong with the 1865 edition, having called at Macmillans on July 15th and inscribed 20 of the presentation copies. It was Tenniel who complained by letter to Dodgson that he was dissatisfied with the printing of the illustrations. So by August 2nd Dodgson had decided to reprint at Clays and sell the first edition as waste paper.

No indication is given as to why Clays were chosen but the reason seems obvious. They were specialists in making electrotypes from wood engravings and expert printers in this medium. They had proved themselves to Macmillans who would have put their name up to Dodgson. Richard Clay immediately put the work in hand, finding it unnecessary to recut the wood engravings as

Dodgson had imagined would be required. On August 11th Dodgson saw proofs, and on November 9th he received his first copy of the new edition (dated 1866, but on sale by Christmas 1865). He declared it: 'very far superior to the old, and in fact a perfect piece of artistic printing'. He then found something better to do with the rest of the rejected edition than selling it for waste. Macmillans received an offer from Appleton's of New York for 'one or two thousand copies'. He and Tenniel agreed, and the Oxford University Press printed 1000 new title pages for the American edition. Mr Bond states that cancel titles were inserted and the books were bound in England, and in this way most of the first edition found its way to America. This conflicts with Charles Morgan's story that 1952 copies in sheets were shipped to America. Mr Bond is not sure either about the forty-eight copies given away.

Dodgson withdrew the edition of 1865 at the instigation of Tenniel who, it is now seen, was protesting about the whole of the printing and not just the illustrations. Mr Bond points out that the typographical layout was marred by 14 'widows' – the occurrences of less than a full line at the top of a page. The correction of this fault by Clays enabled the illustrations to be better placed. These were reproduced a little lighter, making, for example, Alice look prettier. In Mr Bond's paper there are reproductions of illustrations from the 1865 and 1866 editions and the point is fully made. But, additionally, an examination of the 1865 edition reveals that it was set from a 'foul' case, one containing a mixture of normal and condensed characters. 'By contrast,' writes Mr Bond, 'Clays' printing of the second edition was composed in a clean and sharp font, and does not suffer from the defects of a foul case.' The 1865 edition also suffered from bad presswork and set-off ink, which Clay avoided.

No fault was found with the original engravings, which were by the Dalziel brothers. After the blocks had been cut to Tenniel's satisfaction they were electrotyped and were never used to print an edition of the book. Proofs were taken, naturally, and there is a set in Harvard College Library. By using Dr Charlton Hinman's collating machine it was possible to show that the blocks for *Alice* were not redrawn or recut, but there are certainly differences of appearance between them as printed in 1865 and 1866. The most obvious difference is the lighter appearance of the latter, resulting from Clays' better printing technique which avoided both the excessive pressure and the over-inking which characterised the earlier edition.

Mr Bond concludes: 'This experience was a harsh education for Dodgson and it undoubtedly left its mark on his character. From it sprang his notoriously critical attitude towards the production of his later books, the attitude that has been wrongly projected backward and made to apply to the 1865 *Alice*. Dodgson entered upon the venture almost naïvely; he emerged from it rather too thoroughly experienced.'

Once again Clays had shown their superiority as printers, but it is only fair to add that Oxford University Press, renowned today for good printing, was going through a bad period at the time. Its later Printer, Horace Hart, who presided from 1883 to 1915, would have sacked on the spot a compositor who set from a 'foul case'. Clays continued to print *Alice* and many thousands of copies issued from their works.

Macmillans were one of Clays' best customers and relations were always close. When, in 1889, Clays took the then daring step of installing a telephone, they rented it from Macmillans rather than direct from the telephone company. The books printed for Macmillan covered a very wide range. There was a strong religious element – the works of Frederick Maurice, C. S. Vaughan and Archdeacon Farrar – but the educational side was also strong – books on electricity, physics, mechanics, chemistry, mathematics. Medical books were also printed and an oft-told printing legend was also applied to Clays. When Sir Benjamin Ward Richardson's *Field of Disease* was being printed Joseph Taylor is reputed to have gone to Macmillans' manager and implored: 'For heaven's sake get it off the press. Our staff think they have all the diseases in the book.' Novels and lighter fare were also printed – including *Tom Brown's School-days*, *Daisy Miller* and *The Europeans* by Henry James, and others which are now forgotten. The *Life of Milton*, *Malthus and his Work*,

Cobden's *Speeches* all emerged from the Bread Street Hill presses as did the *Memoirs of Daniel Macmillan.* One of the most attractive productions was a two-volume limited edition (500 copies dated May 1st 1879) of *The Poetical Works of Robert Burns*, edited and with a biographical memoir by Alexander Smith, printed on special paper made by John Dickinson.

Clays were now major book printers and particularly of stereotyped editions. Both plaster and papier mâché processes were used up to 1900, when the papier mâché process eventually superseded the plaster cast stereos on the advent of J. M. Dent's Everyman Library series. Clays' services were used by all the leading publishers – George Bell, Bentley, Constable, Chatto & Windus, J. M. Dent, Duckworth, Hodder & Stoughton, Heinemann, Jarrolds, Longmans Green, Mills & Boon, Routledge, Sidgwick & Jackson, Ward Lock, Warne and Williams & Norgate, as well as by firms the names of which have been forgotten except by specialists in publishing history. Possibly the biggest publisher–customer of all during the half century to 1900 was Chapman and Hall, many editions of Dickens' works being printed by Clays.

Surviving lists of stereotyped plates indicate a wide interchange between publishers and printers. A publisher would have a book set and stereotyped by Clays but perhaps printed elsewhere; or Clays would receive stereos from another printer. One publisher would take over another and the stereotyped plates would be a valuable asset. In this case, however, imprints had to be watched and there are various notes warning that a particular set of plates now belonged to another publisher. Lord Stanhope's revival of stereotyping certainly assisted the wide distribution of books but it set many problems for the bibliographers of nineteenth-century literature. A few 'standing orders' still exist, giving instructions about the particular requirements of publishers. For G. P. Putnam of New York it was essential that the plates be shaved to absolute conformity of thickness or otherwise the English publisher or printer would be charged the cost of re-shaving. The United States was a market for stereotyped plates and a number of instructions concern the supply of plates to America.

While most of the books were case-bound, there was growing up a new type of popular publisher, such as George Newnes, for whom Clays printed cheap paper-bound editions. This firm was also to prove a source of business in periodical printing and it is now time to turn to this aspect of the Clay history – one which they eventually abandoned in favour of book printing alone.

NOTES

1. *The House of Macmillan* 1843–1943 by Charles Morgan, London: Macmillan & Co. Ltd. 1943.
2. Ibid.

One of the smaller press rooms at Bread Street Hill

CHAPTER EIGHT

Periodical Printing

RICHARD CLAY II DIED in May 1890, at the early age of 51, leaving a widow, three sons and four daughters. His two elder sons, Richard III and Cecil, aged 26 and 24, were working in the family business as company secretary and deputy manager respectively. The youngest son, Archibald Gregory, was only eight years old. Members of the Cambridge family were on the board of directors, one always acting as chairman; and the brothers were fortunate in having at Bungay, from 1892, a strong manager in the person of J. C. Archibald. The period ahead of them was one of great expansion but one with correspondingly large problems. Cecil Clay, who served the firm for no less than 63 years (1884–1947), saw many changes before his death in 1953.

Although they were not aware of it at first, Clays had to face up to the problems inherent in periodical publishing and printing. Miss Jessie Robbins, one-time London representative (director 1948, retired 1957 and died 1959) wrote some notes on the firm, and of the period 1888–90 she remarked: 'In general there appeared to have been considerable dealings in publishing ventures, and the period covered is chiefly remarkable for the insolvency of a number of customers, payment by Bill appeared to be the order of the day, and much of the Board's time was taken up in dealing with requests for further credit.' She had drawn attention to the main distinction between publishing and printing in the periodical field. Many of those capable of editing and publishing did not have sufficient capital, and printers who had equipment were either not capable or not interested enough to publish – although they were sometimes forced into it. Moreoever, those publishers who were capable, lucky or wealthy tended to become their own printers. Indeed, they were often the only ones with both enough money and the necessary captive printing to be able to invest in the increasingly expensive equipment needed for mass production of popular periodicals – a tendency which became stronger when the photogravure process was introduced.

Clays had a taste of this tendency as early as 1869. They were approached by W. L. Thomas, who wanted to bring out a rival to the *Illustrated London News*, to be called *The Graphic*. It was recognised that this would be a major undertaking and Clays were prepared to instal specially three double-feeder Wharfedales to cope with the production. That these were not ready at once is shown by a note in the Preface to Volume Two of *The Graphic* (July–December 1870), which reads: 'Among other improvements two new Printing Machines, exhibiting great skill in their design and of great power, have just been completed and are now in working order. By their aid the Engravings will be printed in a better style and with greater speed than heretofore.' Additionally, as has been noted, Clays installed the Mackie composing machine to assist in the setting of *The Graphic*.

Thomas was right in his estimate that there was room for another illustrated news magazine. The printed result had a profound effect on the public of the day. News was illustrated with large wood engravings, some of them across two pages, showing, for example, the Cabinet at work. These engravings were so large that they had to be made in several pieces and bolted together. Great skill was required in their preparation and the printers had to use equal skill to print them. However, so successful was the magazine that the proprietor decided after October 19th 1872 that he would print it himself and Clays, for the time being, lost the benefit of their initiative.

Simply as printers Clays had no means of assuring the success of a periodical even if, as in the case of the *English Illustrated Magazine*, they were part-owners. This was an example of the fact that no matter how good the printing or how developed the illustration technique if the content of a magazine does not appeal to a sufficient number of readers it will fail. On the other hand, periodical printing provided highly desirable regular work which could not be ignored. Clays therefore repeatedly faced the dilemma of wanting to prolong the life of a periodical without wanting to take over the publishing side. Cecil Clay's friend of later years, J. S. Elias (who was raised to the peerage as Lord Southwood) solved the problem by taking over periodicals which could not pay their printing bills and thus transformed the small printing firm of the Odhams brothers into the giant periodical publishing house, Odhams Press.[1] Perhaps Elias was fortunate in not being inhibited by a printing background but the Clays had been brought up in the craft and had no taste for journalistic enterprise. Nevertheless, they tried out many different approaches before abandoning periodical printing.

One way was to offer a publisher something special in the way of equipment. The acceptance of their estimate in November 1890 for printing the *Illustrated Sporting and Dramatic News* depended on the installation of yet another new printing machine, for which the board had to pass a special resolution. In January 1905 when Clays were appointed printers of the famous *Illustrated London News* itself, yet another arrangement was made. The printing took place not at Bread Street Hill but near the publisher's office in the Strand – in Greyhound Court, Milford Lane. The arrangement was a compromise. The employees were Clays' but the machinery was purchased by the Illustrated London News and Sketch Ltd. To Clays' board would come all labour matters – requests for holidays, bonuses and donations for 'outings', while the publishers concentrated on editing and distributing the magazine. The printers' wages were listed separately from those of the men at Bread Street Hill and a special banking account was opened. When a new machine was needed the publishers paid for it. During 1907 and 1908 three new Miehles were paid for in this way.

Other periodicals printed by Clays at this period included *The Sketch* (also printed at Greyhound Court), the *Illustrated Sporting and Dramatic News*, the *Lady's Pictorial*, *Our Darlings* and more serious publications such as the *Nursing Times*, the *Fortnightly Review*, the *Independent Review* as well as journals of learned societies and official year books.

A section of the binding department at Bread Street Hill

A mere listing of the publications which issued from Bread Street Hill does not reveal the difficulties involved in acting as printers to a wide variety of publishers. The copyrights which Clays held do not seem to have been acquired deliberately but often in desperation. In the case of non-periodical publications they were fortunate. Cundall's books went on selling, the *Clerical Guide* was a useful property, Meek's local directories were not a burden and even Mr Hogg's life policy which they held against his debts eventually paid off. But periodicals were a different matter. At various times up to 1920 Clays took shares in publishing ventures, such as an electrical trade paper. They lent £1000 and gave extensive credit for a *6d.* magazine to get going; they assisted in *T.P.'s Weekly* and aided famous literary personalities. The *Musical Times* was a constant item of worry and the directors were glad when a rival publication absorbed it. Much of Cecil Clay's time was taken up in attending meetings of creditors or discussions on how periodicals should be kept going.

Perhaps the Clay directors should have thought out their policy earlier but they were never to know when a periodical might turn out to be another *Illustrated London News*; neither could they tell if a periodical might succeed if given an injection of capital and that another might fail. Their approach was erratic and eventually they began to turn down requests for co-operation. In their defence it should be pointed out that they had to keep their employees occupied, particularly later on when they embarked on the building of an ambitious new printing works. Coincidentally with their disillusionment with large-scale periodical printing there came an offer for this works which they gladly accepted. Did the directors but know it it was one of the luckiest things which could have happened to them, but this lies in the future.

Cecil Clay shared the same interest in things mechanical as other members of the family and was also, in his younger days, a regular contributor to the trade press. In the first number of the *Caxton Magazine* in 1901 he noted that, despite all the technical advances which had been made in the printing trade, type was still mainly set by hand. He thought that mechanical composition would cause a more distinct advance in the art of printing than anything else. In fact, Clays, despite their earlier disappointing experiences, could hardly wait for an efficient casting and composing machine to come along, and soon after the Linotype became available in Britain they were making enquiries about an installation.

By 1906, therefore, Clays was one of the most advanced printing firms in the country. In London, eight Linotypes had been installed and the electrotyping and stereotyping foundries were equipped with the most modern machinery, some of it from America. Unusual for the period was a pre-make-ready department where blocks were prepared before going to machine. The large quantities of illustrated letterpress at Bread Street Hill justified the purchase of expensive equipment, which included the De Vinne–Bierstadt overlay process.

There were a number of machine rooms, in the most important of which were seventeen large printing machines, the pride and joy being the new Miehle cylinders. There was also a rotary press – a Marinoni. According to an old employee, when this machine started up it vibrated so much that it turned the beer sour at the local public house, but this may be another printing trade legend.

Because of changes in publishing practice there was now a large bindery at Bread Street Hill. Instead of merely printing the sheets of a book a firm such as Clays would now deliver complete books. The bindery was one of the most modern of its time, being based on mass-production rather than on hand-craft methods. As a consequence, Clays' services were used by most of the leading publishers and this meant that an increasing amount of warehouse space had to be devoted to book storage, which provided another problem for the board to face.

At Bungay, expansion had taken place since Clays took over. The Bungay Press of Childs had been renamed the Chaucer Press, after the Chaucer Society, for which it acted as printer. This society was one of a number founded by Dr Frederick James Furnivall. The earliest of these had been the Early English Text Society, founded in 1864, and which is still flourishing. The work of printing for the E.E.T.S. was considered to be of such importance that a separate 'Furnivall' room was devoted to the composition of the sometimes complicated texts which demanded the use of special type sorts. Dr Furnivall innocently played an important role, did he but know it, in the T. J. Wise 'first edition' scandal, which will be dealt with in a later chapter.

While much of the composition at Bungay was by hand, in 1906 a new 'Linotype' department was designed, and machines installed. Three early models of the 'Monotype' had been tried out but did not apparently meet the demands of the time. Then three keyboards and two casters were installed in 1910 and both systems of composition were used until 1918 when a complete change to 'Monotype' was made.

The foundry had always been an important part of the Bungay works almost since its inception. The plaster cast system of stereotyping had been found useful for many years – up until 1900 in fact and had been used extensively on the E.E.T.S. publications. Combined with hand setting of foundry type the process had its drawbacks. Women were employed in the foundry as 'pickers', their job being to pick out pieces of type which had been plucked out by the plaster. The process was eventually superseded by papier mâché. Electrotyping was introduced at the turn of the century but was not considered very efficient, so that in 1910 the foundry was reorganised on a more modern basis.

There were several machine rooms containing machines of various origins particularly from Germany and America, but the greatest reliance was placed on the Yorkshire-built Wharfedales. As an indication of the evolution of the machine room each American machine was driven by its own individual motor but the others were still driven by overhead shafting.

Only gradually did the bindery expand. This was not due to lack of enterprise on the part of Clays but rather the facts of publishing practice. In the early part of the twentieth century the collating and folding of sheets constituted the extent of the bindery's work. Then in 1905 two wire stitchers, two sewers and a folding machine were brought in. From then on as more demands for binding were made by publishers the appropriate equipment was purchased and Bungay joined London as a complete book manufactory. It had to keep in step with the publishers. For example, only small stocks of cloth were held as binding in boards was still popular and, until the first casing-in machine was installed, this process was carried out by hand by girls.

In 1907 the directors decided to erect an Institute building for the employees at Bungay and instructed an architect to prepare plans. A contract was agreed and a building was erected at a cost of £1990. By late 1908 it was ready to be ceremonially opened. The Chaucer Institute, as it was called, having been built and furnished by the firm was let at a nominal rent of a shilling a quarter to a general committee. Cecil Clay was president, A. P. Hunter secretary, and A. J. Smith secretary of the Reading Room, Lecture and Library Committee. The object of the Institute was to provide facilities for promoting social intercourse, for giving concerts and lectures, dramatic entertainment and dances, organising debates; and 'Ladies and Gentlemen of every shade of opinion' were cordially invited to become members at an annual subscription of five shillings for men and half-a-crown for ladies.

All was ready for the opening which took place on January 6th 1909. Cecil Clay had thought it a good idea to invite leading customers of the firm to be present, among whom was naturally the man who indirectly had given the Institute its name – Dr Furnivall. It should be explained that Furnivall, though in his early life a devout Christian, had become an agnostic, and due to his disagreements with the clerical element in his efforts to improve the lot of working people he was not particularly favourable to religion. He had clashed with the clergy on, among other matters, the question of Sunday sport. At the time of the opening he was nearly 84 years of age and was renowned for his blunt speaking. The event is best described by another valued customer of the firm, J. M. Dent, in his *Memoirs*:

> 'Cecil Clay had asked Dr Furnivall and myself to go down to the opening of an institute which his firm has built for their work-people at Bungay. In the course of his address Dr Furnivall described his attempts with Kingsley and Maurice to get hold of the working-man and make him a scholar. He described in detail the filth the people lived in, the state of the stairs of the model

Chaucer Institute.

LECTURE SEASON, 1912-13

Oct 24, 1912
WILLIAM MILES, Esq., F.R.S.L.
"Dramatic, Humorous, Poetic and Zither Recital."

Nov. 14, 1912
W. H. SHRUBSOLE, Esq., F.G.S.
"Hungary and the Hungarians."

Dec. 12, 1912
REV. GEO. FRANK PACKER,
"Africa."

Jan. 23, 1913
ARTHUR B. MALDEN, Esq., F.R.G.S.
"A Holiday in Switzerland" (with living pictures).

Feb. 27, 1913
CHARLES LOCKITT, Esq., M.A., B.Sc. (LONDON).
"When Woman was Queen."

April 3, 1913
Miss GERTRUDE BACON.
"Flying Machines, Balloons and Airships."

Each Lecture will commence at 8.30. Doors open at 8.
Numbered Reserved Seat Tickets for the above series,
* Members, **3/-** Non-Members, **5/-**
* Transferable only to Members.

Plan may be seen and Seats booked at H. W. Short's, Market Place, or remittance may be sent by post to Hon. Secretary, Library and Lectures Committee at the Institute.

The Chaucer Institute lecture programme for the winter of 1912–13

THURSDAY, JANUARY 23, 1913.

ARTHUR B. MALDEN, Esq., F.R.G.S.

(of the Regent Street Polytechnic, London.)

ILLUSTRATED LECTURE

ENTITLED

"A HOLIDAY IN SWITZERLAND"

(the Playground of Europe.)

The Lecture will be Illustrated by One Hundred **Nature Photographs,** and a series of unique **Animated Pictures** with special series of Winter Sports—Ski-ing, Musical Chairs on the Ice, &c., &c.

Projected by the Polytechnic Cinematograph.

Mr. Arthur Malden, who is paying his second visit to the Institute, is the son of Mr. J. Malden, F.R.G.S., who for nearly thirty years was celebrated in both London and the Provinces for his unique Dioramic Entertainment.

Last Season's Lecture by Mr. Malden was the most popular of the Course and the Central Hall was crowded. Early booking for above is therefore desirable.

There will be exhibited at the close of the Lecture a Selection of the latest

POLYTECHNIC ANIMATED PICTURES.

Details of one of the lectures – the hall was usually filled to capacity

> lodging-house and the stench, etc., and compared it with the present day. And then he began to inveigh against the way in which some people kept Sunday. He advised the workers not to be inveigled into church on a Sunday by a lot of mouldy parsons, but to go out on to the river and the moors and take some exercise and get air into their lungs. He declared it was a waste of life to spend it in church listening to outworn doctrines. Now as the room was full of church- and chapel-going folk, with a fair sprinkling of parsons, it began to empty, and you could feel boiling indignation working up amongst the audience. It fell to me as the next speaker to throw oil on the troubled waters.'

Dent was right about the church and chapel element – many of the Clay employees, in fact, held church and chapel office. Dr Furnivall died the next year and the Clay directors magnanimously sent five guineas to his memorial fund and Cecil Clay was one of the subscribers to the Furnivall memorial book, published by the Oxford University Press.

The Institute provided valuable social and cultural facilities for the people of Bungay. It does to this day, but in 1909 in what was undoubtedly something of a backwater it was an unusually enlightened move on the part of the Clay directors. In the first year debates were conducted on 'Free Trade versus Tariff Reform' and on 'Women's Suffrage', a fortnightly dance was held and other activities included football and billiards, whist and amateur dramatics. Very valuable was the Reading Room, where no less than 10 daily papers and 32 weeklies were available. Two monthlies and a bi-monthly, *The British Printer*, could also be consulted. The facilities even included 'private baths' (bath – threepence; towel and soap – one penny).

In October 1907 John Clay's eldest son, John Hamblin Clay (born 1884) joined the firm. In 1911 he was to join the board of directors and later succeed J. C. Archibald as manager at Bungay. In 1911, too, Archibald Gregory Clay, younger brother of Richard III and Cecil, joined the board. John Clay's younger son, Barnard Augustine (born 1886) joined the staff in 1911 from Cambridge University Press but did not take up a career in printing.

As a new venture lay ahead – the building of a large London factory, which will be described in the next chapter – at this point it would be as well to summarise the position of the Clay business.

They were among the most eminent of book printers, even receiving orders from America (for example – two handsome volumes of Lenôtre's *Romances of the French Revolution* for Brentano's of New York in 1909). While they had to give extended credit to some of the most famous names in book publishing they were generally paid. In the field of periodical publishing the situation was not so clear. They printed some of the most popular periodicals in the country, but were also plagued with troubles arising from the weak capital structure of much of the periodical press. What has not perhaps been sufficiently stressed is that with all this work they were also very big general printers, having printed for such bodies as King's College, London, since the founder's day. Their imprint was found on a wide variety of institutional printed matter – for Christ's Hospital, Marlborough College, the Church Building Society, Soldiers' Daughters' Home, Blackheath School, Dulwich College and the Incorporated Law Society, to choose a few customers at random. In addition, they could not help but be City of London printers. They were not only situated in the City but had close connections with various customers – the nearby St Nicholas Cole Abbey, for example, or their own ground landlord, the Ironmongers Company. The printers in the City (now considerably declined in number, and growing less yearly) took it for granted that work would come from the multifarious activities of the world's financial centre, and Clays were no exception, even if some of the work was small and not very profitable. Hence they printed for the various schools in the City, the livery companies, Sion College, churches and financial and business houses.

The time was not far distant when they would have to make a decision as to what kind of printer they wanted to be, and the new building venture hastened the day.

NOTE

1. See *Viscount Southwood* by R. J. Minney. Odhams Press Ltd. 1954.

CHAPTER NINE

Brunswick Street

THE BREAD STREET HILL premises had never been designed as a printing works and after eighty years of occupation had become too cramped for the volume of business being carried out by Clays. In September 1907 there had been some discussion on the desirability of obtaining new premises, and an offer was made for a block consisting of 171–181 High Holborn and 192–193 Drury Lane, but it was withdrawn in March 1908 on an announcement that the property was to be auctioned.

In preparation for a change to bigger premises Cecil Clay was sent to America in the May to study new methods. In the June the firm had an offer from Mr George Riddell of a site in Brunswick Street, Southwark, and by July 28th they had reached agreement with him to purchase a 99-year lease. It meant pulling down existing buildings and putting up a new factory at an approximate cost of £40,000.

The firm's troubles were just beginning. There were prolonged negotiations over sewers, legal actions arising from the pulling down of the buildings and even considerable delay in getting the lease. Disagreements with architects and builders followed and by November 1909 very slow progress was being made. However, a year later matters were advanced enough for the directors to take the risk of ordering up-to-date equipment for the new works. It took nearly two years to build the factory and in early 1911 arrangements began to be made for moving some of the Bread Street Hill machinery and selling that which was not required. In the March the now Sir George Riddell granted the lease and a flag and a name plate were purchased as a gesture to confirm that the factory was at last ready for occupation. The removal was gradual in order not to disturb the printing of various publications but by the end of the year it was complete.

While a splendid printing works had been erected it had to be paid for and so a loan was raised with the Norwich Union Life Insurance Society and shareholders also contributed. All might have been well if the Bread Street Hill premises could have been let at once to provide some income, but this proved to be difficult.

The accumulated records and plant at Bread Street Hill could not be taken to Brunswick Street and so a mass of archives was destroyed, and venerable industrial relics, such as the Mackie composing machine, were broken up. A few historic records – on which this history has relied – were saved by some far-sighted person, but because further destruction took place on the move from Brunswick Street in the early 1920s, a great deal of interesting material has been lost. The directors cannot be blamed for this – the space required to store the records, if kept, would have been prohibitive from an economic point of view and it is doubtful if, at the time, there were those sufficiently interested in industrial archives to have provided a home for them.

During the period of negotiation over the new factory and the consequent difficulties Clays received an unexpected blow from another direction. On July 6th 1909 they received notice of the termination of their contract to print the *Illustrated London News*. They expressed their regret to the publishers and tried to obtain a renewal by explaining about their new rotary presses expected to be installed in the new factory. However, this was a case where a different printing process was involved and even the tempting offer of advanced letterpress printing could not meet the challenge.

When the young Bruce Ingram first took over the *Illustrated London News* it was printed letterpress and occasional colour supplements, printed by either photogravure or lithography, were included. The expense of the photogravure plates, in particular, was high and the delay irritating – a plate took up to six weeks to produce, but the effect on the public was so gratifying that Ingram insisted that the production situation be improved. He was also convinced that there was no reason why colour photogravure should not be suitable for printing the whole paper. He therefore made enquiries about experiments in France and Germany. While he was in Paris he sent his manager ahead to Germany to which country he was summoned by a telegram. He was to go to Siegburg, near Cologne, to see a photogravure machine. So impressed was Ingram that he ordered a similar machine for the *Illustrated London News*. This 'Rotogravur' press was installed in the Ingrams' own premises and continued in use as late as 1947. This did not help Clays. They were by no means unaware of the other printing processes as they had bound in the supplements printed by gravure and lithography, but they could not offer Bruce Ingram what he required.

As early as November 1908 Clays made the first of a number of moves to enter the field of lithographic printing. They went into business with Fortescue Wetherman & Co., of Enfield, buying a new lithographic press in the process. By the next year it was found that all was not going well and injections of money were demanded to keep the company going. No more is heard of this venture.

In order to gain a satisfactory amount of work for the new factory Clays entered into a syndicate with the University of London Press, for which they became official printers – by taking shares, in effect they obtained preferential treatment with printing orders. Cecil Clay joined the board of the U.L.P. and, in return, J. Y. W. MacAlister joined that of Clays. It was not a happy arrangement. There was slight trouble at first about the transfer of printing contracts which was settled, but for ten years there was little equilibrium and arbitration was frequently called for between the two parties.

In February 1911 when they knew that the new factory was in its final stages the board set about arranging to let the Bread Street Hill premises, but by the next year no tenant had been found. Various offers were made for part of the buildings which were considered unacceptable. In November 1912 Greenaways, the City printers, became interested but nothing concrete was agreed. Finally, in October 1913 Sprague & Co.'s offer was accepted and an agreement was completed in January 1914. So for three years Clays had had to keep Bread Street Hill empty.

The *Illustrated London News* incident had made an impression on the directors and they considered the whole question of photogravure. One big customer – Newnes – expressed interest and in March 1914 the general principle of buying what was called an 'intaglio' machine was adopted. The problem remained as to where to buy such a machine and following Bruce Ingram's example one was ordered from Germany – from the Tiefdruck Syndikat of Berlin – a particularly unfortunate decision as war was to break out with Germany within months. For Newnes Clays printed such magazines as *The Strand*, *Wide World*, *Woman at Home* and *The Grand*.

Before the outbreak of the war there was a great deal of activity and it is significant that Clays were considering not only new printing techniques but also new binding ideas. In July 1914 they purchased a 'Perfect' binder from Sheridan's at a cost of £2060. This is an early example of a firm deciding to bind books with adhesive only, without thread or wire. With an eye to the future the board also began to buy land at Bungay for extensions to the works there.

The outbreak of war hit Bungay initially more than London because while practically every book publisher suspended work on books, the war created an extra demand for illustrated periodicals. Various decisions had to be made by Clays including the question of payment of wages to men in the forces, and even at that early stage insuring against bombs from 'aerial craft'. 'Business as usual' was supposed to be the motto of industry, and Clays tried to live up to it even if some of their customers did not. They did not cancel the order for electrical equipment for the 'intaglio' machine although it was never to turn up; and they also ordered new Monotypes and a Camco folder.

As the 'intaglio' machine could obviously not be expected from Germany new discussions took place with Newnes, and another compromise type of agreement was made by which Clays would buy an 'intaglio' machine in Britain and Newnes would be responsible for the cost of the 'etching plant'. There is no record that the machine was ever installed.

Newnes were successful periodical publishers, but others were not doing so well and once again Clays found themselves making special arrangements for those who owed them money. They now firmly declined to back new publications. At the same time when a publisher wanted something special in the way of equipment they were always willing to oblige. In 1915 a fount of 'long primer' and Monotype matrices were obtained at the special request of the magazine *Land and Water*.

Increases in wages meant that prices had to be stepped up. Most publishers agreed, although it made the situation worse for others. The accumulation of financial worries led to an unprecedented step for Clays in November 1915 – the directors gave themselves notice that they were on one month's engagement only. As trade improved this was revoked in May 1916. The difficulties in relation to shortage of work gave way to those arising from shortage of labour. Bungay, in particular, had difficulty in getting new apprentices. German-made equipment, such as arc lights – began to wear out and replacements had to be sought elsewhere, and, although paper was not officially rationed, supplies were becoming harder to obtain. Money had to be paid out in advance to build up stocks for the periodicals.

On March 20th 1916, John Clay, who had been chairman for eleven years, died suddenly. He was succeeded by his brother, Charles Felix.

At last the end of the war brought daylight and further expansionist moves were contemplated. Since there were no signs of a photogravure press Newnes made another proposal in December 1918. They would be responsible for obtaining a new rotary machine and Clays could gradually buy it from them. This proposal received the support of J. M. Dent who said he could use the machine for his 'Everyman's Library'. Accordingly, a Goss rotary was ordered in June 1919 and a new foundry was planned.

With an eye to the future Cecil Clay paid another visit to America to see what had been going on during the war years. A thousand pounds was paid out in 'Peace' bonuses to the staff and a hundred guineas was donated towards Peace celebrations at Bungay. All was set for the brave new world.

The German photogravure machine continued to be elusive and

so the firm put in a claim under the Treaty of Peace Order of 1919. To their gratification they received a cheque through the Enemy Debts Clearing Office in March 1921 for the machine ordered in 1914, amounting to £971. 5*s.* 2*d.* (£750 they had put down for the machine, plus interest, less commission to the Clearing Office).

In August 1920 the Goss rotary was expected any day, the foundry was being built and the directors were making their plans when suddenly an offer was made, through solicitors, for the purchase of the plant, machinery and premises at Brunswick Street for the sum of £232,500. Clays could not find out who the principals on the other side were, and since they refused to disclose their identity and since they could not satisfy the directors as to their ability to complete the contract the matter was dropped and the draft contract filed.

In September, however, Mr Neal, the solicitor, attended a Clay board meeting to say that Cecil Clay had seen Mr Charles Humphries and it had been agreed that Clays should not be called upon to cancel any printing contracts before the purchasers had paid the money and completed the purchase. So it was agreed to proceed with the sale. The prospective purchasers had revealed themselves and the Clay directors could see that the sale might solve many of their problems, not the least of which was the payment of the loan to the Norwich Union.

On October 20th 1920, the purchasers said they wanted to leave a considerable portion of the money on mortgage. They agreed that Clays should carry on the business for six months, the purchasers to pay all outgoings. An allowance would be made for conducting Bungay business on the premises. The slow progress of the negotiations disheartened the directors when again, suddenly in November, Mr Edward Iliffe of Coventry and his solicitors, attended a meeting at which it was proposed that Mr Iliffe should take assignment of the contract with Dr Gordon Reeve and enter into a direct covenant with Clays. It is not certain whether Dr Reeve and Mr Humphries were partners with Mr Iliffe in this venture but it is not of importance because, in the long run, Clays found they were dealing with Mr Iliffe, one of the important periodical publishers of the day.

On December 13th 1920 an extraordinary general meeting of shareholders was held where it was agreed that the offer made by Iliffe and Sons Ltd., of Coventry and London, to purchase for the sum of £232,500 the premises and plant at Brunswick Street and to take over the unexpired contracts of the company as far as they were carried out at Brunswick Street be accepted. Iliffes also agreed to take over works in progress and the floating stock at valuation. On the 22nd of the month the board agreed to the destruction of ledgers and similar books up to the end of 1913. Two days later a notice went out to the trade to inform that Iliffes had purchased the premises at 1–10 Brunswick Street, with type, plant and fixtures as from January 1st 1921. The staff of Richard Clay & Sons Ltd. were remaining so that there would be no break in the continuity of services and that the directors of Richard Clay & Sons Ltd., had agreed for a period to assist in the management. The business was to be conducted by Iliffe & Sons Ltd. under the name of The Cornwall Press Ltd., 1–6 Paris Gardens, SE1. Brunswick Street was to be renumbered and renamed Paris Gardens by the London County Council as from January 1st 1921.

In February 1921 the board agreed to destroy all old private ledgers prior to 1888 and all balance sheets in manuscript. In August they decided to destroy old and obsolete agreements and eventually they rid themselves of the annoying University of London Press agreement – Hazell, Watson & Viney taking it over. It remained merely to rent a London office at Blackfriars House, New Bridge Street, and all was set for the new era at Bungay. But not quite . . .

There were unfortunate arguments over preference shares and difficulties with Cornwall Press over stocks, but eventually everything was smoothed out. More land was bought at Bungay, a war memorial was unveiled to the twenty-six who had died in the service of their country, and some equipment and type was purchased from Iliffes for the Chaucer Press.

A collective sigh of relief may have gone up from the board after the solution of all the problems which had beset them for ten years, but it could not have been known to them what future difficulties they were avoiding. The evolution of periodical publishing and printing deserves its own history but there is no intention of delaying the Clay story to provide it; but the inner contradictions of this form of enterprise remained often below the surface after Clays had left Brunswick Street – particularly during the years of the Second World War and the period of paper rationing. Only when full competition was restored in the late fifties did the full extent of the malaise become apparent with the melancholy procession of closures and amalgamations of periodicals and periodical houses.

CHAPTER TEN

Thomas J. Wise

NO HISTORY OF the firm of Clays could avoid dealing with the case of Thomas J. Wise (1859–1937), at one time President of the Bibliographical Society; a member of the most exclusive society of book-collectors, the Roxburghe Club; honorary Master of Arts of Oxford University; Fellow of Worcester College; owner of one of the finest of private libraries; forger and thief.[1]

In 1934 Clays printed for Constable of London and Charles Scribner's of New York a book entitled *An Enquiry into the Nature of Certain Nineteenth Century Pamphlets* by two young booksellers, John Carter and Graham Pollard. The contents startled literary and bibliographical circles by demonstrating that some fifty esteemed first editions of various Victorian authors were fakes. While the investigators showed the close association of Thomas J. Wise with these spurious publications they did not actually name him as the creator. They proved that he was involved in the promotion and marketing the fakes but the evidence that he manufactured them was at the most circumstantial, despite the investigators' private belief that he was the culprit. Even so, it was made clear in the book that Wise must know the identity of the forger, and that some explanation was necessary.

There was a certain mild irony in the fact that Clays were asked to print the exposure, as the investigators demonstrated that the fabrications had been printed by Clays. During 1933 Graham Pollard had been in touch with the firm, who had co-operated in the enquiry as best they could. The evidence was that they too were privately convinced of Wise's guilt although they could provide no written orders from him.

From 1882 to 1906 Wise had carried out a programme of printing works of collected authors. It began in a legitimate fashion, but by about 1888 he began to utter forgeries of first editions. One of these, Swinburne's *Siena* ('1868') was noticed by contemporaries in the 1890s and Wise therefore abandoned straightforward forgery because it was too dangerous – a forgery could be compared with the original. His later, more advanced technique was to take some suitable piece from a published volume or periodical and print it in pamphlet form with an earlier date, the implication being that the author or a friend had produced a small private edition before the first public appearance. Collectors were therefore provided with a desirable item which could not be checked against another copy. The grand collectors of the early part of the nineteenth century were not necessarily concerned with the first printing of a book, but the new school which arose in the latter part of the century saw a particular virtue in possessing the very first printing of a work by a famous author, no matter how modest it may have been. But such collectors needed guidance, and here the second part of the Wise plan showed considerable ingenuity. By various means and by the use of dupes he gave his fabrications an air of respectability in bibliographical reference works and then secretly launched them on to the market.

Although the science of bibliography was not very advanced at the time of the creative forgeries there were those who suspected what was going on, but little publicity was given to their views at the time. Suspicion lingered on into the 1930s, but it was left to Carter and Pollard, using modern techniques of paper and type analysis, as well as textual evidence, to show that certain pamphlets could not possibly have been produced at the time of the date in the imprint. Taking, for example, the most important of the group – Elizabeth Barrett Browning's *Sonnets from the Portuguese*, dated 1847, the investigators showed that the paper on which it was printed contained chemical wood, which was not available for paper-making in England until 1874.

While the textual investigation showed, in some cases, that the forger had used a later text than the real first printing, thus condemning the work on that ground, the evidence of the paper was often conclusive. In itself, however, this did not narrow the investigation sufficiently to a particular printer, and so an analysis of type was also undertaken. Here Carter and Pollard were in the position in which scientists sometimes find themselves. It is possible to check laboriously every possibility in some field of research but following up a presentiment will often save time. The investigators could have conducted a comprehensive search of the work of a number of printers, but they had learned in 1932 that copies of the suspicious pamphlets turned up regularly in the catalogues of a bookseller named Gorfin. Gorfin turned out to be Wise's former office boy and the stocks of pamphlets had been sold to him by Wise. They also knew that Wise had been personally, and as secretary of the Shelley Society, responsible for publishing facsimile reprints of the work of nineteenth-century authors, which were printed by Richard Clay and Sons Ltd. So they turned to these first, with satisfactory results.

Sixteen of the suspect pamphlets, including the *Sonnets*, were found to be set in a 'modern' type face, which normally would have two 'kerned' letters, in the lower case. A 'kerned' letter is one in which a portion of the face extends beyond its body and this thin projection is exposed and fragile and has the disadvantage of breaking off, necessitating the renewal of the type. But the particular fount was found to have a kernless 'f'. This indicated setting from 7 to 38 years later than alleged because the investigators could find no 'kernless' design in a modern face before 1883 in typefounders' catalogues. Another typographical feature of the *Sonnets* was a question mark of a peculiar form. It was obviously a wrong fount and such a hybrid would necessarily be restricted to one printer only. An examination of *Alaric at Rome*, by Matthew Arnold, a type facsimile of the original edition of 1840, edited by Wise in 1893, revealed a kernless 'f' and 'j' and the odd question mark. It was also noticed that the text of a type facsimile of *Alastor*, 1887, and the notes to the type facsimile of *Hellas*, 1886, were also set in this fount. Clays were responsible for the printing, and they were therefore asked what the origin of the fount was. It transpired that it was cast by Clays in 1876 from matrices supplied by P. M. Shanks & Son Ltd., and called by Clays No. 3 Long Primer (although it was

Shanks's Long Primer No. 20). It was used until 1893. In about 1880 Richard Clay II, the inventor, tiring of the breaking of kerned types tried to manufacture a kernless 'f'. Not succeeding, he asked Shanks to make it for him. They also made a kernless 'j', and these two special characters were substituted between 1880 and 1883, the first use which the investigators could discover being in the *English Illustrated Magazine*, number one of October 1883, which Clays printed. The kernless design was made by bending back the main stem of the 'f' and 'j' so that the centre of their terminal curves came into the same perpendicular line as the main stem itself. This makes the letters look as if their backs are broken, the design resembling a button-hook.

The question mark was a different matter. It was not that sold by Shanks for the fount and was clearly a 'sport' from the matrices of some other type face. It was a Bourgeois face (approximately nine point) cast on a Long Primer (approximately ten point) body and was, moreover, an italic face set upright. It appears that when Clays broke or lost the correct question mark matrix they supplied the deficiency by casting the italic question mark of the next smaller size upright on the body. This was a curious thing to do as it would have been simpler to have obtained a replacement matrix from Shanks. The resulting question mark was out of place and its incongruity was recognised, presumably by Wise, on at least one occasion. Mr Pollard has pointed out[2] that the *Siena* forgery, which was set in Clays' Long Primer No. 3, has quite a different question mark. There are fifteen question marks in the thirty-six nine-line stanzas and they are therefore a noticeable feature of the typography. Mr Pollard conjectures that another question mark must have been substituted deliberately to make the forgery look more like the original. Clays' Long Primer No. 3 could be identified without the odd question mark, but *Siena* has additionally been identified as Clays' work independently of the fount. On a copy of the forgery in the Bodleian Library there are traces of set-off, deciphered as being from a King's College prospectus and, as noted, Clays were the College's regular printers. The substitution of the question mark does not mean that Wise had a particularly wide knowledge of type or that he had an inkling that the Long Primer would betray him 40 years later. It simply underlines the fact that he was alert to the danger of comparison between original and forgery, leading him to change his tactics later.

In all, thirty-seven of the pamphlets investigated were printed in one or another of only three text types, the remainder in a variety of others, which were shown to have been used in Shelley Society publications. There was one printer who held all the types – the Shelley Society's printers, Richard Clay & Sons Ltd.

Wise received his first direct intimation of possible exposure in October 1933 when Pollard called on him and asked questions about the pamphlets. Wise decided to take advance evading action. He tried, without success, to silence Herbert Gorfin, his former office boy, now a bookseller, through whom the pamphlets had been marketed; and then turned his attention to Clays. The authority for this is Wilfred Partington, author of *Forging Ahead* (New York, Putnam, 1939), expanded into *Thomas J. Wise in the Original Cloth* (London, Robert Hale, 1946). He describes an interview between Wise and Cecil Clay (which, he says, Clay confirmed as accurate) in which Wise asked: 'Can't you say you had nothing to do with these things?' – meaning the pamphlets. Cecil Clay replied: 'How can I when you know we printed them for you. Aren't you rather giving yourself away?' The interview terminated quickly. Then, early in 1934, Wise wrote a letter to *The Times Literary Supplement* altering his earlier published account of how the key forgery, the *Sonnets*, had come into his possession. He now stated that it came from Harry Buxton Forman (who had died in 1917). This was one of a series of attempts to pass the authorship off on to a former friend, who, it is now thought, may have actually been involved.

When the *Enquiry* was published Wise once again tried to blame the forgeries on to others, all conveniently dead. However, Viscount Esher, in a letter to *The Times Literary Supplement* of August 23rd 1934, summed up the feelings of his fellow-collectors who had bought copies of the pamphlets for large sums of money, when he demanded a full explanation from Wise as to how he came by them.

This was followed by a letter from Wise's wife in which she claimed that Wise's doctor had forbidden him to carry out any public correspondence.

Under the pressure Wise resigned from the Roxburghe Club, giving as his reason 'ill health'. He died in May 1937. Since that time investigations have been carried out which confirm that Wise was undoubtedly the fabricator not only of the pamphlets condemned in the *Enquiry* but of others, and that he was guilty of other misdemeanours, including, for example, selling books to America with misleading or false information and the theft of leaves from early seventeenth-century books of plays in the British Museum.

Wise had his supporters, and one of them inadvertently set off a chain of events which revealed a document which condemned Wise in his own hand. A New York bookseller, Gabriel Wells, wrote a pamphlet entitled *The Carter-Pollard Disclosures* (New York: Doubleday, Doran & Co. Inc. 1934) in which most of the defence was based on Wise's obvious wealth and position. Wells carefully avoided tackling the detailed evidence of the *Enquiry* but could not resist a gleeful additional sheet to his pamphlet when he discovered that the investigator had mistakenly attributed an article to Wise instead of to Forman. It proved nothing except that a small error had been made, but it caused Carl H. Pforzheimer, a book collector, to recall that he had proofs of the article, and in checking up on them he came across a damaging letter from Wise to Forman admitting fabrication of Tennyson's *The Last Tournament* (falsely dated 1871), which had been proved a forgery on grounds of paper, type and text.

However, had they but known it, the two original investigators had picked a vital pamphlet when they chose *Alaric at Rome*, Wise's reprint of 1893, to study type and imprint. For while this was a legitimate article, Wise had imprudently used the same type to produce a forgery of the 1840 edition. He must have suppressed this indiscretion for only three copies have so far been found – two which Wise sold to Americans and one in the library of a friend. Only in 1936, well after the *Enquiry* had been published, was one of the copies discovered. If the identical type in facsimile and forgery and the provenance of the forged copies had been noted in 1933–4 there would have been direct evidence that Wise was the forger.

Although they had assisted the investigators, the directors of Clays were naturally in a difficult position when the *Enquiry* was published. They thought privately that Wise was guilty but owing to the wholesale destruction of records over the years they had nothing to prove the guilt. Wise had certainly been a customer of the firm, but even if correspondence had been preserved it is unlikely that it would have included incriminating reference to the forgeries. Wise was too cunning for that. The Forman letter is probably not typical. He was goaded into his written indiscretion by Forman's criticism of his methods of numbering limited editions.

However, it is well-established that Wise was closely connected with the Browning and Shelley Societies, and he made no secret of the fact, so that references to these societies in the few surviving Clay records may provide a clue at least to the way Wise's mind was working.

A 'Case Signature Book 1877–1885' records composition work for the Browning Society from 1881–4. On the two latest pages devoted to the Society are interesting notes: 'Average of 25 proofs sent out, 4 pp. at a time' and 'Average of 25 proofs of each Paper sent out'. This number of proofs, large enough for a special note to be made, may have been genuinely necessary, but perhaps Wise, who was involved with Browning Society publications from 1884, was already thinking ahead. The usual practice would be for the top set to carry the printer's stamp, but the others might suggest raw material for small booklets, without a contemporary imprint. The Schedule of 1887 confirms that three Shelley Society publications which were never published were actually set by Clays. The fact that it was decided not to publish them did not stop Wise having a copy of each run off to provide rarities for his own library. They are: *The Necessity of Atheism*, *Posthumous Fragments of Margaret Nicholson* and *A Letter to Lord Ellenborough.*

A small entry in the Schedule shows that Clays' employees do not seem to have differentiated between Wise in his various capacities. His own 'privately printed' *Letters to Elizabeth Hitchener* is listed under the Shelley Society. This was one of a series of volumes of Shelley's letters, some of which, including these, he was not entitled to publish. So that while the schedule dates the composition of the Hitchener Letters for 1887 and proofs in the University of Texas Library bear Clays' date stamp of 1887 and 1888, the volumes did not actually appear until 1890, when Wise felt the owner of the copyright might cease to make trouble. More significant, however, is the fact that the proofs in the Texas library include a title-page with a New York imprint dated 1886 – indicating that Wise was already contemplating false imprints. His piracy of *Poems and Sonnets*, reprinted from Dowden's *Life of Shelley* (1886), took the matter a stage further. This was published under the fictitious editorship of Charles Alfred Seymour (i.e. Wise) and under the equally fictitious imprint 'Philadelphia', 1887. In the 1920s Wise admitted that the book was printed by Clays. It is considered to be Wise's first piracy, to be followed in the next year, 1888, by the first forgery – Elizabeth Browning's *The Runaway Slave* ('1849'). To date Wise is believed to have been responsible for 20 piracies and 62 forgeries.

The attitude of the Clay directors in not naming Wise may be open to criticism, but it followed that of the investigators themselves, and seemed to them to be the only one they could adopt under the circumstances. They therefore refused to be pushed by the Secretary of the First Edition Club, A. J. A. Symons, into making public statements. In an article in *The Book Collector's Quarterly*, July–September 1934, Symons asked: 'How did it happen that these printers gave the forger such blind obedience as to leave their own name off their wares, and put false dates on imprints instead?' He continued: 'So far they have offered no explanation, and after reading a proof of the present article, Mr Cecil Clay, writing for the firm, has 'no comment to make'. Messrs. Clays' present attitude is very disappointing, but on the other hand they seem to have given Messrs. Carter and Pollard considerable help in the beginning of the investigations.' Clays were perhaps well advised to be wary when dealing with Symons. According to Percy Muir[3] Symons was engaged in an attempt to protect Wise by undermining the *Enquiry* evidence if he could, or by producing another candidate as forger.

In any case, a partial explanation had, in fact, been given on page 65 of the *Enquiry*: 'The facsimiles which they printed for the Browning Society, the Shelley Society and for private circulation by Mr Wise were all printed on separate sheets from the prefatory matter or notes. There is nothing on the actual leaves of these facsimiles to show that they are reprints; and from their having already done work of this sort, it follows that Messrs. Clay would not have regarded the request for the name of another firm and a false date in the imprint as necessarily involving any malpractice on the part of their now unidentifiable client.' It might have been added that it was not entirely necessary to make a request since the Clay employees were used to setting copy with strange imprints for facsimiles not only for Wise but for other publishers.

The reason why Clays were deceived into producing the Wise fabrications becomes apparent when the nature of their quite legitimate business with Furnivall's societies is considered. Because of Wise's connections with certain of these societies it was almost inevitable that Clays should have been used as his printers – and no other firm. That is not to say that Wise did not print elsewhere in his lifetime, but Clays were a necessary factor in his special programme of forgery.

Wise started business life as an office boy to an essential oil merchant in the traditional commodity market area of the City of London. He made progress and later was considered one of the shrewdest of buyers and, no doubt, built up a modest fortune. He began to collect rare books at an early age and to join literary societies, giving the impression that he was a wealthy young businessman. In reality, he was a moderately paid clerk with an expensive hobby, and he needed money to build his collection. The production of facsimiles for the Shelley Society gave him the idea of producing false first editions which could be sold for a profit.

Wise's descent to illegitimate enterprise was fairly rapid, but the brilliant idea of fabricating non-existent first editions did not come at once. From 1882 onwards, private printings, unauthorised publications and piracies led downward to forgeries and then to complete fabrications. In 1882 he had a limited edition of his own verses printed by William Fullford, of Pentonville Road. Later in the year he joined the Browning Society (founded by Furnivall the year before). Then in 1884 Wise tried his hand with a reprint of Keats's *Ode to a Nightingale*, which Fullford printed for him in an edition of 29 copies. This was the last time he used Fullford's services as in the same year his election to the committee for the Browning Society involved him in the Society's publishing programme and hence with Clays the printers. It was decided to move the Society's printing from Clays' works in Bungay to Bread Street Hill in London. This may have been a coincidence but it was so convenient a move to Wise that it might even have been engineered by him. The closeness of his City office to Bread Street Hill could have been a determining factor in moving the work there. It obviated the necessity of correspondence to Bungay and allowed verbal instructions to be given.

Clays were involved with Furnivall in the first place because they were the successors to John Childs and Son, of Bungay, whose services were used by Furnivall and his associates. The choice of this country printer is not so strange as it might appear. Childs was often in London soliciting work from publishers and came of a family with pronounced radical and anti-Establishment views, which would appeal to Furnivall. Moreover, the firm was advanced technically for the time. The famous *Transcript of the Registers of the Company of Stationers*, 1554–1640, was nearly all printed at Bungay. It was originally an 1870 project of the Early English Text Society, and was to be edited by Furnivall and C. J. Rivington, Clerk of the Company, but the Society had so many texts in hand that the Council transferred the project to Edward Arber, with whose name it is now always associated. Between 1875 and 1877 four volumes were printed by Childs & Son, although as Clays took over at Bungay in 1877 they actually finished off the fourth volume. Volume V was printed in Edinburgh. Thus it was that Clays inherited the printing of the Early English Text Society's publications, some of which were particularly suited to repeat printing by stereotyping. While Furnivall did not use Clays exclusively, nevertheless he was well disposed towards them for they had done him the honour of naming their works after his Chaucer Society and maintained a special composing room for the difficult texts he asked them to set. By about 1880 he had definitely appointed 'Messrs Clay and Taylor of Bungay' as official printers. It was therefore natural that Furnivall should use Clays for the work of his newer societies and that the printers extended their trust for this old and valued customer to his associates, who included Wise. Wise did not choose Clays as his printers; they were chosen for him.

When Wise began to use Clays it was as an emissary of the Browning Society and he was well established with the London staff by the time such figures as Cecil Clay came to play any important part in the firm's affairs. Cecil Clay recalled to the investigators how Wise would come through the main door, tipping his hat to Clay or others present, and go straight through to the head clerk, J. R. Maylett (later London manager), to whom he would give his instructions. Maylett's connivance in Wise's schemes has therefore been presumed, but owing to the peculiar nature of the work done for Furnivall's societies he may simply have been deceived by Wise. Clay also mentioned to the investigators that Wise's account was always paid up to date. In fact, in the schedule of 1887 there is an outstanding sum in the name of T. J. Wise of £16. 18*s*. 0*d*. This is the only reference to Wise so far found in Clays' surviving records. There is also an entry 'A. Forman . . . £11. 2. 0*d*.', but this may have no significance. The Shelley Society ran up a large bill for £632. 11*s*. 8*d*. Partington mentions a larger sum, but also states that it was paid off by individual members of the Society, including Wise.

Wise did not come to Clays as a stranger requesting the printing of some literary matter with a false imprint, but as the representative of Furnivall, who was well known to the firm, and with jobs such as a type facsimile of Browning's *Pauline* (1833) a legitimate undertaking to please members of the Browning Society. Having set for Mr Wise in 1886 a title-page dated 1833, a compositor would think there was nothing untoward in setting the date of Elizabeth Browning's *The Runaway Slave* (one of the forgeries) as 1849. It might be thought that Wise took a risk in marketing as valuable first editions pamphlets which at least a small group of printing craftsmen knew had been composed contemporaneously. But, in fact, the risk was small. Few £2-a-week craftsmen collected rare books and in the unlikely event of one of them seeing an entry in a bookseller's catalogue he would have to have seen the actual copy before realising that it was in a familiar typeface. It would have been disastrous for Wise if, by accident, one of the Clays had happened to be a collector of, say, Browning's works but all the evidence suggests that the interests of most of the family were more technical and sporting than literary.

To sum up, Wise got away with his forgeries for some 40 years because bibliographical specialists in the main were not technically minded and because the printing craftsmen with whom he worked were accustomed to printing sheets of literary matter with odd imprints for respectable literary societies. They could be excused for thinking that Wise continued to be an officer of such societies for, despite the fact that the Shelley Society ceased functioning in 1892, Wise continued to use the Society's printed writing paper, with himself named as honorary secretary, at least as late as 1897.

Wise was caught because two young booksellers decided to risk their reputations and cut through the veil of suspicion about a group of pamphlets, on which some of their colleagues were making a good profit; because Richard Clay II became tired of kerned letters breaking and because Wise was greedy. If he had not continued to sell batches of the suspect pamphlets to Gorfin well after he was financially secure, the world might never have heard of the Wise scandal.

The firm of Clays may have been embarrassed, bored or both over the years by the unflagging interest in this scandal, but if it is any satisfaction to them there cannot be a librarian or bibliographer of standing in the English-speaking world who does not know their name.

NOTES

1. It is not the purpose of this chapter to deal with the whole Wise saga, which interested readers may follow in the existing extensive literature and that which, no doubt, will continue to be published. A certain amount of background is necessary, but the main object has been to examine the part which Clays played in the case. It is particularly not concerned to speculate on whether Wise had any collaborators although, as mentioned, there is evidence that H. Buxton Forman was involved. Clays have no recollection of doing business with Forman. Other books, besides those mentioned in the text, which provide valuable information include: *The Firm of Charles Ottley, Landon & Co.* by John Carter and Graham Pollard (London: Rupert Hart-Davis; New York: Charles Scribner's Sons, 1948); *Books and Book Collectors* by John Carter (London: Rupert Hart-Davis, 1956); *Thomas J. Wise and the Pre-Restoration Drama* by D. F. Foxon (London: The Bibliographical Society, 1959); and *Thomas J. Wise Centenary Studies*, edited by William B. Todd (Austin: University of Texas Press; Edinburgh: Thomas Nelson & Sons Ltd., 1959). The *Centenary Studies* also contains guidance to many other publications which relate to Wise.

2. Graham Pollard; *The Scope for Further Typographical Analysis* in *Centenary Studies*.

3. Percy Muir: *Minding my own Business* (London: Chatto & Windus, 1956).

THE CLAY

THOMAS C
(1726–

J

ELIZABETH JANE CLAY

CHARLES JOHN CLAY (1827–1905) = EMILY JANE EADY

EMILY SUSAN CLAY

MARY ALIC

RICHARD CLAY (1864–1935) = (1) HELEN MARSH (née GILL)

HELEN STELLA CLAY

= (2) JANET HICKS

ARTHUR CECIL CLAY (1866–1953) = HEL AN KNU

ALIANORE KATHLEE CLAY

RICHARD CLAY (b. 1909) = THEODORA MARY CORSINI

MARGARET PHILLI

RICHARD SIMON MILES CLAY (b. 1940) = HEATHER WESTNEDGE

BRIDGET GERALDINE CLAY

RICHARD CRISPIN CLAY (b. 1971)

BELINDA SOPHIE CLAY

OLIVER M

MARY AIMEE CLAY

MARIAN EMILY CLAY

JOHN CLAY (1858–1916) = MARY HAMBLIN SMITH

ALICE CLAY

C

HILDA MARY CLAY

JOHN HAMBLIN CLAY (1884–1957)

BARNARD AUGUSTINE CLAY (1886–1933)

EMILY GABRIELL CLAY

FAMILY TREE

.AY = ANN BARKER
3)

)HN CLAY = MARY HODGES
:758–1841)

ICHARD JEREMIAH CLAY = SUS
(1789–1877)

: CLAY

RICHARD CLAY = M
(1839–90)

NA
IE
SSON

CONSTANCE ETHEL
CLAY

M

N

MARJORIE CLAY

A CLAY

.ES EDWARD CLAY
(b. 1975)

IARLES FELIX CLAY = ETHEL A
(1861–1947)

ELLEN

RICHARD OWEN
CLAY
(1908–31)

Aerial photograph of the present works

CHAPTER ELEVEN

Development at Bungay

THE WORKS AT Bungay had been quietly expanding since the end of the 1914–18 war and once the directors were free of London in 1921 they began to buy more land for development so that the basis could be laid for the emergence of the Chaucer Press as a major book-printing firm. More 'Monotype' casters and Miehle presses were installed and the foundry was expanded. The electricity installation was modernised and the directors turned their attention to such matters as 'improved sanitary equipment' and a technical library for the case room.

The list of customers in the 1920s reads like a roll-call of all the great names in British publishing. Among the biggest were Macmillans, Chapman and Hall, the S.P.C.K., the Religious Tract Society, Ward Lock, the British and Foreign Bible Society, and Dents. J. M. Dent obviously thought Clays was the firm where a newcomer to publishing could learn about book production, and he asked in June 1923 if his grandson, Martin, could study at Bungay. It was agreed that he should come for six months, as from October 1923. In the April of the following year, after the term was up, J. M. Dent wrote a letter thanking the directors for having given his son an insight into printing.

Clays had not yet, however, become complete book specialists. They were still very much general printers with a miscellaneous list of customers. In their accounts in the twenties are many tiny items. An extreme example, it is true, but one which will indicate the kind of work carried out for small organisations, is the African Society. At intervals Clays printed forty-eight notices for nominations to the Council and posted them for £1. 16*s.* 0*d.*, printed Annual meeting cards for 17*s.* 6*d.* and addressed envelopes, inserted cards and posted them for £1. 1*s.* 0*d.* Apart from the lack of profit, a multiplication of this kind of job could prove harmful to the smooth running of large-scale book production. But many of the societies concerned had been friends of Clays right back to the first Richard, and it was a delicate matter to refuse their work. Cecil Clay, in particular, liked to keep up the old contacts.

The post-war boom soon ended and Clays had to take a number of extreme financial measures to keep going, but keep going they did in a period of increasing unemployment. They were fortunate to be able to do so, as small publishers were going bankrupt with distressing regularity. Some were allowed to pay off their debts in small sums, but Cecil Clay began his rounds again attending liquidation meetings and arranging to prop up firms which had some potential.

There is one point to bear in mind about the Clay directors – they never ceased trying. Determined to keep abreast of the times they decided once more to break into the lithographic field. In 1924 they paid a deposit of £300 on a new factory in Barnet, paying another £2700 on completion. They spent another £3500 on plant and formed a company called Phototype Ltd., with a capital of £10,000, to make lithographic plates. Almost at once there were difficulties. Somebody had forgotten to check the electric current and it cost £542 to get the North Metro Electrical Co. to convert A/C into D/C. Phototype Ltd. was a constant subject of discussion at board meetings. In July 1925 another £1500 had to be invested. By 1931 the directors gave up the struggle and sold the business to Swains. What happened exactly to the earlier lithographic business is hard to say but with regard to Phototype Ltd. there are those who remember its activities and, in general, it is conceded that the plates made were of a high standard but the whole process of offset lithography had not advanced sufficiently at that time for such a supply firm to be successful.

In 1926 the firm suffered a loss when Archibald Gregory Clay died at the early age of 43. He left a six-year-old son, John Marshall Clay. The eldest Clay brother, Richard III, died in 1935, but his son Richard (born 1909), after training at the London School of Printing, had joined the board in March of that year.

The General Strike of 1926 did not affect Clays unduly. On May 19th, the Manager at Bungay laconically reported to the board that the employees had come out on strike on May 4th in connection with the General Strike throughout the country and had returned to work at 8 a.m. on May 18th.

The period until the late thirties was one in which the gradual change away from general printing to book production speeded up. Nearly all the machinery purchased was towards this end.

In 1935 a publisher called Allen Lane, unable to persuade his family firm to publish soft-cover books, familiarly known as 'paperbacks', started his own publishing business, Penguin Books Ltd., for this purpose and set off a revolution in British publishing and book production. This was to have a profound effect on Clays, who were called on to print some of the first 'Penguins'.

While in Europe there was a long-established custom of issuing books in paper wrappers which could be rebound according to taste, the paperback, as known today, has as its ancestor the German Tauchnitz, editions of works written in English, intended primarily for the British traveller on the Continent, and not for sale in Britain. Although there had been experiments in paperback publishing in Britain it was Allen Lane who really attacked the market with his 'Penguins' at *6d.* a copy. His venture was frowned upon by other publishers and booksellers were not enthusiastic. After a hesitant start the success of 'Penguins' was assured.

A further development was also planned – no less than a link-up which would provide a London base for Clays again. Discussions had started in 1938 with the object of amalgamating Clays with Noakes Bros. Ltd., a well-known London firm of process engravers, which had been incorporated in June 1928, and which had absorbed various other firms of the same kind, such as Badoureau & Jones, Burlington Engraving, Carl Hentschel Ltd., and Marshall Engraving.

At an extraordinary general meeting on July 27th 1938 by special resolution Richard Clay & Sons Ltd. wound itself up to give effect to a scheme of amalgamation with Noakes Bros. Ltd., at the same time registering a company called Richard Clay and Co., Ltd. A newly named company, Clay-Noakes Ltd., was incorporated on the

14th July 1938, with directors from each of the participating companies. Cecil Clay was named chairman in the agreement and R. B. Crewdson managing director. Then on July 25th, by special resolution, the name of the company was changed to Richard Clay & Co., Ltd. The reason for the involved action was that it had been desired that the new company should bear the name of Richard Clay, but the shareholders of Clays had to pass a special resolution to consent to this, and Clay-Noakes Ltd. was used temporarily until this could be effected.

In 1939 conscious of the inadequacy of the machine room and bindery at Bungay to cope with the rising amount of book production the directors decided to reorganise thoroughly these two departments. Memoranda were prepared on the structure of the machine room, the machine power necessary if production continued to rise, and the capital required to rebuild, re-equip and reorganise the machine room so that in 1940 it could execute the current turnover at least cost.

The same was done for the bindery, and ambitious rebuilding plans were prepared for these departments and in consequence for the whole Bungay plant.

Despite the fact that it was founded in London the firm of Clays does not seem to have been lucky in its ventures there since leaving Bread Street Hill. Once more a war intervened, and all the hopes held out for the new London firm were dashed. The Noakes factory was an early victim of the war. Affairs went steadily enough in the latter part of 1939, after the declaration of war, but in the air raids of 1940 and 1941 the factory and equipment were completely destroyed. R. B. Crewdson resigned as a director in March 1940 (he died in 1942). Only by August 1944 was a small department started up again after months of unceasing effort by Cecil Clay and F. W. Price. The start was not auspicious. After many weeks a few rooms had been equipped, but on the morning that work was due to start the fourteen journeymen and two boys arrived to find that a V2 bomb had dropped near by. The damage caused by the bomb was cleared up and the firm began to work again. It continued as a subsidiary of Clays until early in 1950 when it was sold to The

Amalgamated Press. By a curious coincidence, as in the case of the Cornwall Press, which was originally owned by Clays, by a series of amalgamations Noakes Bros. is now part of the International Publishing Corporation.

The Forces had claimed the two younger Clays, Richard IV and John Marshall, and gradually, as the Noakes Bros. directors resigned, the board became depleted. To strengthen the board J. M. Clay was elected a director in 1944, although he was still in the army.

In 1943 a meeting of the Bungay employees had taken place in the Mayfair Cinema, as the Chaucer Institute was not available. The meeting was addressed by Cecil Clay. Charles F. Clay, at 82, was not able to make the journey from Cambridge, and Richard Clay was a prisoner-of-war in Germany. It was left to Cecil Clay therefore to announce a profit-sharing scheme, the essence of which was as follows: when wages, rents, rates and taxes and all other outgoings of the business, including interest on debentures, had been met, and when reserves carried forward and sinking funds had been provided for, a sum available for distribution remained. This would be used in the first place to pay a dividend of 6 per cent on the Cumulative Preference Share Capital and any arrears, and 7 per cent on the Ordinary Share capital. Then any further sum available for distribution would be divided equally between the shareholders and the wage earners. The share of the wage earners would be distributed among those who had been employees during the preceding financial year in proportion, and as an addition to the total amount of remuneration received by them respectively during the year. This scheme was known as the Chaucer Press Charter. The difficulties of trading under war conditions precluded any spectacular payments to the employees but with the return from the Forces of key men production and profits began to soar and the amount paid out by April 1950 totalled £38,797.

A Joint Advisory Council was established in 1944. This met monthly, and was made up of representatives from each department. Constructive suggestions were made as to the efficient running of the works and a number of useful ideas were put into effect.

In 1946, as a result of representations made through this Council, a special issue of employees' shares was made available. These were issued and redeemed at par and were not transferable.

Demands for reading matter during the war from defence and armed forces meant an enormous increase in the production of the easily-handled paperback book. In December 1939 Allen Lane had proposed to Clays that they print and bind £30,000 worth of 'Penguins' a year – at the average rate of 50,000 copies of three books every fortnight with a margin for reprints. This was a major operation. Wartime conditions necessitated the reception of 600 tons of paper -- approximately enough for 4 million 'Penguins' – at the rate of 15 tons a week. Special preparations had to be made for storage and not only the Chaucer Institute but the warehouses of other firms had to be called into use.

Printing and binding plans were worked out. The foundry was instructed to be ready to make 400 curved and flat plates a week. Printing and folding machines were to run night and day to handle 80,000 'Penguins' a week. Internal organisation was so planned that there should be no hold-up in production; a works sheet showing the position of a 'Penguin' was to be sent every Monday to the Production Manager of Penguin Books. Once the continuous flow of 'Penguins' began it was not to be stopped to allow other work to be pushed through on machines allocated to 'Penguins'. Thus the beginnings of a highly mechanised mass book production plant were now apparent.

Richard and John Marshall Clay had returned from the services – Richard in 1945 and John Marshall in 1946 – and in the June 1947 *Chaucer Press Review* Richard Clay outlined his views on future technical developments. These were mainly concerned with the development of electronic devices. His ideas about lightweight type made of plastic, weighing less than a third of metal type, and consequent economies, were not so wide of the mark for the time. In fact, type of all kinds now tends to be by-passed by filmsetting.

A major event occurred in September 1947 when Cecil Clay retired from the firm after 63 years of service. The employees and the printing and publishing trades joined in paying their tributes to one who was considered to be a model employer. He was succeeded as chairman by his cousin, John Hamblin Clay, and Richard and John Marshall Clay became joint Managing Directors at Bungay. John Marshall Clay was appointed Town Reeve of Bungay in 1952, being the fourth holder of this office from the Chaucer Press. His predecessors were S. Fiske, a reader (1927–8), H. E. Bowerbank, Director and Works Manager (1935–6), and W. Courtney, Bindery Manager (1949–50). Mr Clay shared with Mr Bowerbank the distinction of proclaiming the accession of a new monarch – Mr Bowerbank of Edward VIII and Mr Clay of the present Queen. Richard Clay was President of the East Anglian Master Printers Association from 1952–3 and Chairman of the Book Printers Section of the British Federation of Master Printers 1955–6.

CHAPTER TWELVE

Corporate Growth – the Post-war Years 1945–77

by RICHARD CLAY IV

THE TASK OF recording the development of Clays from the end of the Second World War to the present time has fallen largely on me, and as it was my privilege to be closely involved in the summit running of the Company from 1945 to 1976 together with J. M. Clay and others. I am happy in my retirement to try to record events as I see them in retrospect.

The remarkable achievements and indomitable spirit of Cecil Clay have already been chronicled, but tribute is also due to those others who helped to guide the Company through the very difficult years following the destruction of the London factory of Noakes in 1940: A. D. Newbery, who managed the Company's finances so admirably and died suddenly in 1946; H. E. Bowerbank, who ran the works at Bungay throughout the war years and soldiered on although a sick man, also dying shortly after the end of the war in 1946; P. N. Davies, who in addition to assisting A. D. Newbery, and later becoming Company Secretary, was also responsible for a major part of the Company's sales; and Jessie Robbins, surely one of the most remarkable sales persons the trade has ever known.

As a result of wartime bombings and general shortages, book publishers found themselves almost totally denuded of stocks, and the demands on printers were almost unlimited. There was therefore no shortage of work, and the problems Clays had to face were how to find the equipment and manpower to meet the demand. As demobilisation proceeded there was a gradual return of men from the forces, but these, it must be remembered, had left as youths and returned as adults, married with children, and their prime necessity was somewhere to live. So desperate was the housing shortage that the Company was forced to spend an enormous amount of time and money on locating and purchasing almost anything which had four walls and a roof, including a number of properties which had previously been condemned. At one time, after modernising such properties, the Company was the owner of over 130 dwellings, but even this number did not satisfy more than about fifty per cent of the demand, and the Company was plagued by labour shortages of one sort or another for a good many years.

During 1945 and 1946 much of Cecil Clay's remarkable energy was devoted towards rebuilding Noakes Bros. Ltd., the process-engraving subsidiary which had been destroyed by enemy action early in the war, and the peacetime rehabilitation of the plant at Bungay was left largely in the capable hands of H. E. Bowerbank, with Richard Clay the IVth, and later in 1946 J. M. Clay when he was discharged from hospital. However, between December 1946 and July 1947 a number of sad but sweeping changes were to take place which drastically altered the construction of the Clay Board. Firstly, H. E. Bowerbank died on December 19th 1946, to be followed three days later by A. D. Newbery, who died on December 22nd. In February 1947 C. F. Clay, now in his eighties, also died, and in July 1947 Cecil Clay resigned from the Board after serving the company for sixty-three years. This left the management ball very firmly in the court of the two younger generation Clays. Happily, the running of the London office could be safely left in the capable hands of P. N. Davies, who had been appointed to the Board in 1945, assisted by Miss J. Robbins, who was appointed to the Board in 1947. The running of the Noakes Bros. process-engraving subsidiary was largely left in the hands of F. W. Price, its managing director, who had also been appointed to the Board of Clays in 1945, following the resignation in 1944 of Mr R. S. A. Noakes, who had joined Cecil Clay after the blitzing of the London factory and performed valuable services to the company during the war years.

On the retirement of Cecil Clay, J. H. Clay, although no longer actively engaged in the running of the business, took over the post of Chairman, where his many years of experience and the wisdom of an older man gave invaluable support to the comparatively inexperienced younger generation. Despite the great efforts of Cecil Clay, R. S. A. Noakes and F. W. Price, the process-engraving subsidiary which they had fought so gallantly to rebuild was never really a commercial success, and in 1950 this was disposed of to The Amalgamated Press and F. W. Price resigned from the Board. Thus, for the first time for a great many years the Company found itself in the position of being able to devote all its energies to the business of book manufacturing with no outside distractions. Financially the company was now in very good shape, and in the five years from the end of 1945 to the end of 1950 net pre-tax profits increased from £38,000 to £97,000. Reserves had been built up from nil to £125,000, and about £200,000 had been invested in new plant and buildings. In fact, much of the 'new' plant was second-hand, as delivery dates for new equipment were being quoted at anything from three to seven years, and it was quite impossible to wait that long in order to try to satisfy the tremendous demands for our products, but thanks to the Herculean efforts of our engineering staff, all sorts of machinery was brought into useful productive operation, and output of hard-cased books increased from under two million to just over four million in the five years, and of paperbacks from just over one million to two and a half million.

Looking at the Company's position today, the 1950s emerge clearly as the formative years during which the company concentrated its efforts towards increasing its productive capacity on the paperback type of book in accordance with market demands. Output of hard-cased books remained largely static during this period at around four million copies, whereas paperbacks increased from two and a half million to eight million six hundred thousand in the same period. The 1950s also produced several other changes which were to have a significant effect on the Company's later growth and development. Firstly, in November 1951 the Board was fortunate in securing the services of F. W. R. Douglas, who was senior partner in the stockbroking firm of Fielding, Newson-Smith & Co., and his wide experience both commercial and financial in fields other than printing was to prove of immense benefit to the Board, which was in danger of becoming rather parochial in its outlook. In 1956 J. H. Clay retired and the Chairmanship passed to Richard Clay the IVth, with J. M. Clay as managing director. The year was significant in the history of the Company's development. Firstly, acting on the advice and guidance largely provided by F. W. R. Douglas, the company went public, and for the first time its shares were quoted on the London Stock Exchange, and secondly, the company embarked on a two-year programme of work study and work measurement which involved a substantial financial investment and was to have significant influence on both employee earnings and productive efficiency in the years to come. Thus, at the end of 1960 net pre-tax profits had increased to £234,000 and reserves amounted to £380,000.

Just as the 1950s have been identified as the formative years, the 1960s clearly emerge as the growth years, and it was during this period that the foundations of the present structure of the Group, as opposed to the Company, were laid. Lithographic printing had made tremendous advances in the post-war years, and for some time the directors had been aware of the fact that they could no longer ignore this branch of book production, as it was becoming a serious competitor, particularly in the field of reprints, and in 1961 the Company was able to acquire the old-established family business of Fletcher & Son, Limited, which was conveniently situated in Norwich, only 14 miles distant from Bungay. The Chairman and managing director of Fletchers, J. H. Payne, was then 70 years of age and anxious to retire, and the factory also needed entirely re-equipping to suit the purpose for which Clays required it, and they were fortunate in obtaining the services as managing director of C. G. Birchall, who energetically threw himself into the task of reorganising Clays' latest acquisition. Even so, it was not until 1963 that Fletchers contributed any profits to the Group's earnings.

By 1960 the Company's policy was firmly committed towards the further development of rotary printing, and this in turn resulted in increasing expertise in the production of long-run book work, which apart from paperbacks tended to be concentrated largely in the field of educational textbooks. This left the company ill equipped to compete effectively with an important section of the market for which there was a considerable demand, notably short-run fiction titles, while at the same time it badly needed additional throughput of printed sheets to fully utilise the capacity of the extensive bindery which had been built up.

Still bedevilled by a housing shortage and with skilled labour in short supply, the Company decided to look elsewhere for this additional manufacturing capacity, and in 1963 it purchased the whole of the share capital of Northumberland Press Limited at Gateshead-on-Tyne. Although geographically distant from Bungay, where the sheets would have to come for binding, Northumberland Press had the attraction that it was already specialist in just this field of short-run fiction composition and printing, and it had a young and enthusiastic management team under the managing directorship of D. R. Hale. The company was now able to offer its customers manufacturing facilities covering almost the entire field of book publishing – long runs, short runs, letterpress or litho, and binding in a variety of styles both paper covered and hard cased, and more important, it enabled each manufacturing centre to specialise in the particular field to which it was best suited.

In 1964 both C. G. Birchall and D. R. Hale were appointed to the Board of the parent company, Richard Clay and Company Limited. In 1967 D. R. Hale resigned from the Board to take up a challenging appointment elsewhere, and R. Boyd, who had looked after the company's technical development programme for a number of years, was appointed to the Board as technical director. In 1969 the Board was further strengthened by the appointment of D. A. Peters as personnel director. Thus the company entered the 1970s with the basis of a management team each specialist in its own particular field, in place of the oligarchy which had formed the Board from 1957 until 1964.

By the end of 1969 the investments in the subsidiary companies at Norwich and Gateshead were starting to pay dividends, and production of hard-cased books at Bungay had increased from four million in 1959 to nearly eight million in 1969 and paperback

Site of the present London offices before rebuilding

Huntsworth Mews, the London offices after rebuilding

production had soared to nearly twenty-eight million. Net pre-tax profits had increased to £454,000 and reserves amounted to nearly £1 million.

At the end of 1969 P. N. Davies, having reached the age of 65, retired after twenty-two years as a director of the company, and in 1971 F. W. R. Douglas died suddenly and R. S. M. Clay, the son of Richard the IVth and the fifth generation in direct succession to the Founder, was appointed to the Board. In 1972 J. Dundas Hamilton, a partner in Fielding, Newson-Smith, was appointed to the Board in place of F. W. R. Douglas, and in the same year J. W. L. Nichols joined the Board as secretary and financial director following the retirement, after 20 years valuable service, of S. R. Potter, who had been company secretary and chief accountant. Thus by 1972 the management team was complete and has formed the basis of the company's operation ever since.

There were two other developments in 1970 which are of importance. Firstly, ever since its blitzing in 1940 the Company's London office had been plagued by varying degrees of impermanence in rented properties which for a variety of reasons either proved to be too small or the leases expired, and in 1970 it was able to acquire freehold premises in Huntsworth Mews (just off Baker Street), which was a derelict property requiring almost total rebuilding, which when completed not only provided spacious accommodation for the London sales staff but also for the first time since the disposal of the London business in 1921 gave the Company security of tenure on all its properties, which were now freehold. The other venture was not so successful. With the growth of lithographic printing at Norwich the company felt that it needed to have its own facilities for colour origination, and late in 1969 it acquired a 40 per cent interest in Anglia Colour Laboratories, which was a small business just outside Norwich, which the company set up jointly with others. However, this never became a commercial success, and in 1973 the business was disposed of.

Between 1970 and 1975 most of the Group's expansion took place at the Bungay plant, mainly in the field of paperback production and in further developments in filmsetting and rotary printing, and by the end of 1975 paperback production amounted to sixty million copies, more than double the output in 1970. Production of hard-cased books had increased to eight million eight hundred thousand. In 1975, net pre-tax profits for the first time reached £1 million and reserves amounted to £1,664,000.

In May 1976 Richard Clay IV retired, and J. M. Clay was appointed Chairman. Changes in market demand necessitated a drastic reorganisation of the Northumberland Press subsidiary, and during 1977 the printing activities there were discontinued, and it now operates solely as a typesetting establishment. Also in 1977 the Board was strengthened by the appointment of J. R. Clayton as a non-executive director.

CHAPTER THIRTEEN

Technical Development 1945–77

by RICHARD CLAY IV

PRINTING AND PLATE MAKING

IN 1945, so far as equipment was concerned, there was no immediate problem, as the Company was faced with a position where it had more machines than men to man them, but with an order book which rapidly lengthened to a two-year forward delivery position it was quite apparent that something drastic would have to be done, as it could never hope to catch up using traditional methods. Fortunately for the Company, Cecil Clay, with his usual foresight, had been advocating the use of sheet-fed rotary presses to replace the traditional flat-bed machines ever since the early 1930s, and in 1938 the Company had purchased two old Cottrell sheet-fed rotaries which, curiously, had been used back in 1911 for printing part of the *Illustrated London News*, to which reference has been made earlier. These presses were not a great success, but they did serve the invaluable purpose of indoctrinating the personnel at Bungay into the use of the new techniques required, and following on from this, again with great foresight, Cecil Clay had ordered two Hoe sheet-fed rotary presses in 1943. These two presses were due to be delivered in 1948, but owing to the general dislocation of industry immediately after the war they did not in fact reach Bungay until 1951. As a result of experience with the old Cottrell presses, Cecil Clay had also ordered with the Hoe machines specialist plate-making equipment, designed jointly by Hoes' and Clays' own staff, to produce precision curved plates accurate to one-thousandth of an inch. It says a great deal for Cecil Clay's foresight and the adaptability of the staff at Bungay that these very close tolerances were in fact achieved.

Moulding presses for plastic plates

By the end of 1952 the Company felt sufficiently confident in its ability to make the necessary precision plates for rotary printing that it started to look for the next step forward. Both the Cottrell presses and the Hoes had been single-sided presses, that is, they printed on one side of the sheet only, which meant two passes through the machine to produce a complete perfected sheet, and what we logically required was a perfecting press which would print both sides at one operation. At that time there was not available any sheet-fed perfecting rotary press, but the Company located an ancient reel-fed Derriey machine which, although it had many limitations, did have the correct cylinder diameter for paperback production and also was a perfecting machine. This was installed in 1954 and gave Bungay its first experience of reel-fed perfecting printing. However, the speed was very limited, and the machine was never really installed as a serious contribution to productive capacity, but regarded more as an experimental project, and it was disposed of in 1957. At that time there was no thought in the trade, either among publishers or printers, of rationalising book sizes. Indeed, it was fashionable for publishers to make their books in different sizes to their competitors, and with paper being still comparatively cheap there was really no stimulus to think otherwise. This meant the Company needed to have presses that were capable of printing a variety of different size sheets, and although this presented no problems so far as sheet-fed presses were concerned, the complications of a variable-size web-fed rotary press were formidable. Nevertheless, in 1956 the Company went ahead and ordered two presses, one a variable-size reel-fed rotary press from Fruhwald & Jager, and the other a large sheet-fed rotary perfector from Koenig & Bauer. Both these machines were delivered in 1958, and the sheet-fed machine was an immediate success, and indeed is still used on productive work today. The variable-size reel-fed machine, however, proved to be so complex, and so lengthy were the times required for resetting it for different sizes, that it was finally scrapped in 1961; not the first time in the Company's history that its passion for technical innovation had over-ruled natural prudence. This period really marked the ultimate in the development

One of the Timson presses

of the traditional hot-metal stereotyping process which had so inspired Richard Clay, the founder of the Company, over a century before, but the advantages of the lightweight flexible plastic or rubber plates which had started to become available could no longer be ignored, and from 1958 onwards the Company devoted its efforts towards developing this form of plate.

Rubber plates had been in use in the United States for some time and were a known quantity, in so far as it had already been proved that they could safely be used for over one million impressions without any signs of wear. But they had limitations so far as the reproduction of fine type was concerned, and the Company decided to develop on thermoplastics, which were much newer, and although their printing qualities were established, their ability to stand up to the required number of impressions had still to be proved. To this end a small single-sided sheet-fed rotary press was ordered and installed in 1961, and once this had been used for test runs and the life of the plastic plates had been satisfactorily proved, the Company pressed on and ordered from Messrs. Timson its first specialist reel-fed rotary press for paperback production, which was installed in 1962. This press proved so successful that a second one was ordered almost immediately and installed in 1964, and paperback production leapt from ten and a half million copies in 1962 to twenty-two and a half million copies in 1965.

One again Clays found themselves pioneering a new technology, as they were one of the first, if not the first, to use these plastic plates as a standard product for such a wide range of bookwork, and much of the sophisticated equipment for the manufacture and mounting of the plates was designed and manufactured by their own staff. Thus after a decade of development and experiment the Company had at last developed a technique which has formed the basis of its successful rotary letterpress printing ever since, and for ten years after 1964 all subsequent press installations were based on the use of these very successful plastic plates.

In the early 1970s by which time the Company was firmly established as one of the major paperback suppliers, further platemaking development was to take place. Paperback publishers who had originally concentrated mainly on reprints of popular fiction and classics had been steadily expanding their publishing field and were now producing text-books of all kinds. Also, with steadily rising prices there was an increasing desire to avoid the costly business of resetting the text matter in order to suit the paperback format. These demands could obviously be met by utilising the photographic techniques in common use among lithographic printers, but at that time the overall demand did not appear to justify the massive investment required in order to install a special-purpose web-offset press. There was, however, available on the market equipment for producing photopolymer plates, which is a technique whereby a photographic negative is used to produce a flexible relief printing plate which can be run on the traditional letterpress rotary machine. In 1973 therefore, the Company installed plant to produce these photopolymer plates, and this was an immediate success and served to satisfy the customers' demands. It was, however, realised that this process, although filling a convenient gap at comparatively modest expenditure, had considerable limitations both technically and economically when compared with the full potential of traditional offset lithography, particularly when viewed in conjunction with the Company's steady development in computerised filmsetting. It was also felt that a market existed for illustrated bookwork in longer runs, and in 1974 the Company installed its first rotary press which had the facility for printing both plastic and photopolymer letterpress plates or alternatively, straightforward offset lithography, and this was followed in 1977 with the installation of a second machine of similar design specifically designed for the production of paperbacks.

COMPOSITION

From 1945 until 1952 there was really no significant development in the Company's policy on composition, and all typesetting was done on traditional Monotype hot-metal machines. Efforts to improve the efficiency of the composing department were mainly devoted to improving working conditions and layout and the updating of existing equipment, and it was not until 1952 that two

A section of the filmsetting room at Bungay

Intertype machines were installed. The Company's earlier involvement with slug-setting machines had not been a particularly happy one, and there was undoubtedly a certain amount of bias against this form of composing, and so far as paperbacks were concerned the demands of Penguin, the pioneers, were linked to such a high standard of typography that this could not be satisfactorily achieved except on Monotype equipment. However, at this time the emergence of other paperback publishers who were successfully exploiting a more ephemeral type of book, demanded cost saving in preference to typographical excellence. Once committed to the use of slug-setting machinery, the Company soon devoted considerable energy towards improving the efficiency of this form of composition. It was not long before it had installed its first tape-operated equipment for teletypesetting. Teletypesetting is a system whereby a perforated paper tape is produced on a separate keyboard and is then mounted on the slug-casting machine, which is driven mechanically at very much higher speeds than can be achieved by manual operation. There was nothing inherently new in adopting this technique, as it had been in use for many years on newspapers, but it was comparatively rare to find it used in bookwork.

This was not a particularly successful venture, but it is of some importance, as in its attempts to overcome the shortcomings of the keyboard equipment the Company was stimulated to develop its own electronically operated keyboard, and this really marked the beginning of a continuing development programme resulting in the use at the present day of the highly sophisticated equipment which has proved remarkably successful.

By the early 1960s the development of electronic keyboards had advanced sufficiently for the Company to start looking for the next step forward in improving its typesetting abilities, and in 1964 it installed its first computer in the composing room. This was a machine called the Linasec, which consisted basically of a cathode-ray tube display television screen, a high-speed paper-tape punch and hyphenation function buttons for use by the operator. It had two main functions, firstly, it relieved the keyboard operator of a great deal of decision making as regards end of line and hyphenation, thus improving both accuracy and output. Secondly, it meant that the printer could produce different editions of a book in two or more different sizes of type, different typefaces and different measures without recourse to rekeyboarding the entire manuscript, which hitherto would have been necessary. Clays were the first British book printers to install this equipment, and it is interesting to note that although today's computerised typesetting functions are obviously far more sophisticated, many of the basic principles first commercialised in the Linasec machine are still incorporated in modern equipment. By the middle 1960s, therefore, the Company had successfully pioneered substantially improved keyboarding techniques and mechanisms and had also seen the potential of the use of the computer as an aid to the typesetting function.

There were obvious limitations to the Linasec, as it was only designed for use with slug-setting machines, and in 1968 the Company installed its first filmsetting machine, the Photon 713, which was capable of producing filmset type matter at many times the speed of the old traditional hot-metal machines. So far so good, but the rolls of filmset material pouring out of the Photon machine still had to be corrected and made up into pages, which involved laborious and costly hand work. There appeared to be no viable equipment readily available on the market, so in 1968 the Company drew up a specification and commissioned Elliott-Automation to build a computerised display screen for automating the correcting and make-up functions, many of the programmes being developed by its own staff. This system ran successfully into 1977, when the idea was expanded with a new three-display system which enabled the complete correcting and making up into pages of bookwork material before the actual filmsetting operation. In 1977 the first photo composer, the Photon, was replaced by two Monophoto units.

BOOKBINDING

The Company's advances in bookbinding techniques were largely linked to the development of adhesive technology, and while the bookbinding process was restricted to the use of traditional hot animal glues no real progress could be made in the development of unsewn binding. However, in the early 1950s, with the development of cold polyvinyl acetate adhesives, all this changed and the Company was able to produce increasing numbers of books satisfactorily, both hard cased and paper covered, using this method. Initially, Flexiback machines were used for this work, but with the growth of the paperback market it soon became apparent that something more productive would be necessary, and in 1956 the Company installed its first unsewn binding line solely for the production of paperbacks. This was based on a Martini BBA machine, the first to be installed in the United Kingdom.

The quality of the binding using polyvinyl acetate glues was undoubtedly excellent, but with the Company's steadily increasing involvement in paperback production, the prolonged drying time which cold glue required meant that books after leaving the binder had to be stacked down for several hours before they could be trimmed and packed. With paperback production running in excess of twenty million books per annum this became an intolerable burden, and in the 1960s the Company started to look at hot-melt adhesives which were then being developed. Their ability to set almost immediately on application opened up the development of completely automated binding lines, with the books being trimmed and packed off a conveyor belt in one continuous process. More recently, further developments of hot-melt adhesive technology have enabled the Company to apply the same techniques as it successfully did to paperbacks to its hard-cased binding. Most of these books today are produced on automated lines with no waiting between the various processes.

The successful use of these new adhesives depends largely on the application of strict quality control from raw materials to finished product, and the Company was one of the first to set up a testing laboratory under the control of a qualified chemist, and over the years has successfully developed a number of specialised items of testing equipment, and today the routine checking of paper, inks and adhesives is an essential part of everyday production.

One of the cased book binding lines

SUMMARY OF TECHNICAL DEVELOPMENTS

In a little over a decade therefore the book-manufacturing process at Clays has been through more than one complete technological revolution. In the Composing Room hot-metal composition produced at about four characters per second and laboriously corrected and made up by hand has been steadily replaced by computerised filmsetting at hundreds of characters per second, and the correction and make up is done by white-coated compositors sitting in front of a computer-linked visual-display unit. In plate making the stereotyping process developed by Richard Clay I, and done manually with a pot of hot metal and a hand ladle, has been replaced by plastic plates, which have then been joined by photopolymer plates and more recently by offset lithography. In the Machine Room, seven large web machines have been installed since 1962. More recently the company pioneered a new generation of small high-speed web machines known as 'mini-webs'. Three of these units were installed in 1976 and 1977. For the first time it became economically possible to print orders as low as 1000 copies on reel-fed machines. The combined effect of all this development was to leave only a handful of the forty-two sheet-fed printing machines which the company had in the 1950s.

In the Bindery over 50 per cent of the Company's production of hard-cased books is now done by the unsewn method, and the number of sewing machines, from a peak of some forty machines in the 1960s, is now reduced to under twenty, and paperbacks, which in the late 1940s were all sewn, are now entirely produced by the unsewn method, and some seventy-five million will have been produced in 1977, compared with under two million in 1945.

CHAPTER FOURTEEN

A Portrait of Bungay

by Eric Fowler

BUNGAY IS A handsome little town. It lies inside a loop of the river Waveney, which meanders through a broad green valley between the two fertile counties of Norfolk and Suffolk. At the opening of the loop there are the Castle Hills – earthworks overgrown with grass and trees, and more ancient than the Norman castle, whose remains are now hidden behind the shops and inns of Bungay market place. The castle was once so strong that Hugh Bigod, Earl of Norfolk in the thirteenth century, boasted (vainly, as it turned out) to King Henry II:

> Were I in my castle of Bungay,
> Upon the river Waveney,
> I would ne care for the King of Cockney.

But Bungay now looks as if it had never heard of fortification. It is dominated by the lofty and graceful flint tower of the priory church of St Mary, whose churchyard forms a green in the very middle of the town. And behind St Mary's, in another green yard, stands the smaller, older and certainly not less beautiful Trinity church, with a round flint tower that is probably Saxon.

As for the rest of Bungay, it looks as if it has not changed with any precipitation since that climactic event in local history, the great fire of 1688, which destroyed the old timbered houses and gutted St Mary's church. Thereafter, Bungay restored the church and gradually rebuilt itself in brick and tile, and in a pleasant succession of styles, ranging from the period of Queen Anne to that of the young Queen Victoria.

And so it stands today, with a mixture of streets broad and narrow

The Buttercross – Photograph by G. R. Hawes

(but mostly narrow), radiating from the domed and pillared Butter Cross, and eventually plunging down steep little hills, and over narrow bridges across the river, until they lead into the larger stream of motor traffic that is modern England. Bungay is a little place set apart, on one side by the Castle Hills and on the other by a great common – once a racecourse and now a golf course – that fills all the rest of the loop of the river.

It is characteristic of the town that, instead of a Mayor, it retains the still older, Anglo-Saxon office of Town Reeve. Not unnaturally, this office has been filled several times by Bungay printers. John Marshall Clay, when he was appointed in 1952, at the age of 32, was saluted as the youngest Town Reeve in history.

Bungay is now an urban district of 3700 inhabitants. Not only the residential outskirts of the town but also new houses in the surrounding villages are tacit evidence of the growth of Clays and their staff. And, just off the road to Beccles, there is a huge, anonymous, grey building which looks like an aircraft hangar that has somehow become detached from its airfield. This is Clays' new book store – of the size necessary for a firm that prints more than 70 million books a year.

One might expect that a small town so dependent on a single industry would have 'Chaucer Press' written all over it; but, on the contrary, a visitor arriving in Bungay market place for the first time has to ask where the printing works are. To all appearance, the main business of Bungay is catering for country shoppers; and the subsidiary industries – making sheepskin coats and making cricket bats from willows grown in the Waveney valley – might as well be the staple ones.

Not that the Chaucer Press is far away: it is simply not ostentatious. The works are less than a couple of hundred yards from the market place, down Broad Street. Past the handsome old bank house and the modest local cinema, there presently appears a range of long, low, brick buildings, spreading from the skirts of the town to the edge of the common. Obviously the Chaucer Press, like Topsy, has 'just growed' – according to the needs of the business.

Here is no prestige office block, all plate glass and concrete, set in the midst of a smooth essay of landscape gardening. You pop round another corner – into Popson Street – to find the office. And inside it there are no carpets, no Scandinavian arrangement of indoor plants, no exhibits of abstract art, no elegant bored receptionist. You are shown up concrete stairs into a room furnished with a venerable leather-covered table, upright chairs, two telephones, a steel filing cabinet and a framed plan of the works. The walls are decorated with the Chaucer Press Charter (in Gothic letters, on parchment, and impressively sealed), an engraving of the original London works in Bread Street Hill, and a complimentary address of bygone employees to Richard Clay, jun., Esqre, on the attainment of his majority.

Judging by the style of it, this must have been Richard III, and the date 1885, for they begged the young man to accept the memento of a gold locket, and trusted that 'as you continue to grow in years and understanding you may be better and better able to assist your excellent father in sustaining and extending the good name and well earned fame of the firm'. These sentiments were illuminated by an industrious water colourist with a border of forget-me-nots, the insignia of an hour-glass, a lamp and a book, and the monogram, RC.

For an historian, the waiting room somehow sets the tone of the Chaucer Press. It is obviously used as a work room as well as a waiting room. It takes an historic background for granted, but is far more concerned with the industrious present; and, as a room in which practical men discuss hard facts, it would be incongruous if it were trendy.